CONTENTS

INTRODUCTION

" Fuchsias have become an indispensable part of our gardening. Neither my garden nor countless others would be quite the same without them. And the reasons aren't hard to find: the flowers are very distinctly different from those of anything else you are likely to grow; their colours, while not exhibiting a huge spectrum, are striking and appealing; and, perhaps above all, their flowering period is among the longest of any garden ornamental. My problem in this book has not, therefore, been in persuading you of the value and beauty of fuchsias, but simply deciding how to make a selection of the ten or more thousand varieties and one hundred species. I have inevitably had to limit myself to those that I have seen personally, and have included a considerable number of those that I have grown. Because my own interests lie especially with the species, I have probably included proportionately more of them than might seem justifiable but I do want to encourage more gardeners to try these quite beautiful plants. "

I have described the species arranged according to the Sections of the *Fuchsia* genus in which they lie. The varieties presented more of a challenge, for having made my selection, I decided that simply to arrange them alphabetically, which is the pattern in almost every other fuchsia book I have ever seen, is not really very helpful. I have, therefore, grouped the varieties by colour, choosing primarily the corolla (petal) colour, in the broad categories of white, pink, purple, red, orange and 'others' (mainly blue).

Nonetheless, aside from these broad divisions, describing fuchsia colours is a minefield. The real problems are that the colour range is rather small, the colours change as the flowers age and, with limited exceptions, no-one has attempted to relate the colours to standard charts or descriptions. The descriptions generally used in nursery catalogues are those given by the original breeder; but one man's royal purple can be another's rich mauve; or one person's cardinal red, someone else's deep scarlet. I have tried to rationalise as far as possible by reference to

real flowers and to colour charts but until someone systematically grows every variety in carefully defined conditions and records the colours of each flower, this pretty unsatisfactory state of affairs must prevail.

For each species, I have attempted to give a little of the history of its introduction to European gardens – a fascinating aspect of the subject that touches on the excitement of the botanical exploration of South America. For varieties, I have given the name of the breeder, the country of origin, the date of release and the parentage where this is known or has been disclosed. Accounts of the dates of origin of fuchsia varieties can vary from one reference source to another, mainly because of confusion between the date of the raising or registering of a variety and its availability to the public.

As in other books in the series, I have indicated those plants that have been awarded the Award of Garden Merit (AGM) of the Royal Horticultural Society. While this is not a guarantee that you will succeed with it or even like it, it does at least identify those plants that

have achieved recognition by experts of their garden value, in independently conducted trials.

I have described the flowers of each of my selected varieties in some detail and you will find on pages 8-9 a description of the structure of a fuchsia flower that will make the categories of corolla, tube and sepals easy to understand. I have also given an indication of flower form (double, semi-double or single) and size.

Hardiness is an important although confusing aspect of fuchsia cultivation. All fuchsias are derived from species that live naturally in climates less harsh, and certainly subject to higher minimum temperatures, than prevail in most winters in most European gardens. Nonetheless, some, both species and varieties, will survive outdoors in many places, especially if any pruning is delayed until the spring. In mild areas, some are hardy enough to be used as hedges while in other places, the above ground growth may be killed by frosts but the plant will sprout again in the following year.

There is no universally agreed way of describing the hardiness of fuchsias and so I have adopted the hardiness grades that I have employed elsewhere in this series (see Table on the next page). There is unfortunately no ready way of determining the relative hardiness of a fuchsia by looking at the plant, although relatively few varieties able to survive widely outdoors have large or double flowers.

There is no mistaking a fuchsia; no other garden flower has anything like the same grace and flower shape

Stefan Buczacki

Best Fuchsias

HAMLYN

Publishing Director Laura Bamford
Creative Director Keith Martin
Executive Editor Julian Brown
Design Manager Bryan Dunn
Designer Tony Truscott
Editor Karen O'Grady
Production Clare Smedley
Picture Research Wendy Gay
Special Photography Andrew Lawson

First published in Great Britain in 1999
by Hamlyn
a division of Octopus Publishing Group Limited
2 - 4 Heron Quays, London E14 4JB

© Octopus Publishing Group Limited 1999
Text © Stefan Buczacki 1999
Design © Octopus Publishing Group Limited 1999

ISBN 0 600 59672 9

A catalogue record for this book is available from the
British Library

Produced by Toppan
Printed in Hong Kong

Hardiness grade	Approximate minimum winter temperature tolerated	Practical ability to survive outdoors in Britain in winter
Hardy	-15° to -20°C (5° to -4°F)	In all except the coldest areas
Moderately hardy	-10° to -15°C (14° to -4°F)	In most areas
Fairly hardy	-5° to -10°C (23° to 14°F)	In many areas, especially fairly close to the coast
Barely hardy	0° to -5°C (32° to 23°F)	In very mild areas
Tender	Above 0°C (32°F)	Nowhere

HISTORY AND BOTANY

" The naming of plants is a curious and rather random business. Sometimes a genus is named after the type of locality in which it is found (like Ammophila, *meaning sand-loving), sometimes after some obvious and outstanding characteristic (*Cyclamen, *after the circled, twisting fruit stalk), sometimes modern taxonomy has simply taken over a name that was used in classical times (*Castanea*), and sometimes, it is named after a real person, generally someone who has contributed greatly to the study of plants of this or similar type. The man immortalised in the name* Fuchsia *was none of these things. He was a German herbalist and Professor of Medicine who never saw a fuchsia or anything significantly resembling one. For Leonard Fuchs died in 1566, 137 years before Père Charles Plumier, a French priest turned botanist and explorer, published a book called* Nova Plantarum Americanum Genera, *in which he described the plant we now call* Fuchsia triphylla. *Plumier collected this, the first fuchsia species to be seen by a European botanist, on the island of Hispaniola in what is now the Dominican Republic during the third of three expeditions that he made at the end of the 17th century on behalf of Louis XIV. Plumier named all of the new plants that he found after earlier botanists and Fuchs simply drew a lucky straw. "*

Plumier himself was lucky because *Fuchsia triphylla* is a bit of an oddity in occurring on Hispaniola; *Fuchsia* is almost entirely a genus of the western side of Central and South America, with some curious and fascinating outliers in New Zealand and Tahiti.

That is no evidence that Plumier collected any seeds of the 'three-leaved fuchsia with red flowers' that he described but within the succeeding 20 or 30 years, Philip Miller at the Chelsea Physic Garden in London had both acquired seeds and raised plants to flowering although they were subsequently lost.

Other species were discovered in the wake of the first report and *Fuchsia coccinea* from Brazil was in Britain by 1790 and a Chilean species with red, short-tubed flowers, *F. lycioides,* by 1796. They were joined in Europe in the early years of the 19th century by other important species including the small tree-sized Mexican *F. arborescens* in 1824, the hugely significant and hardy *F. magellanica* around 1823 and another Mexican, *F. microphylla* in about 1827. The stunning, long-tubed *F. fulgens,* also Mexican, came in 1830 and the glorious Peruvian species *F. corymbiflora,*so easy to raise from seed and with elongated, vivid red flowers, followed in 1840.

Fuchsia fulgens and *F. magellanica* were very probably the first two species to be hybridised in England and the variety 'Standishii', in 1839, was among the first results. Gardeners and nurserymen began using others among the early species too. They crossed and re-crossed, always seeking, as nurserymen do, something that nature alone had never managed. Really significant advances came in 1840 with 'Venus Victrix', the first variety to combine a blue-purple corolla with white sepals and tube, and, in 1855 with 'Queen Victoria' and 'Mrs Story', the first double fuchsias with a white corolla (all of the early hybrids had single flowers).

There were other interesting developments too. Variegated foliage appeared in a number of forms from the mid-18th century onwards and although it's a characteristic that seems to have gone from favour, at least one very early variety, 'Sunray' (page 78), is still obtainable. Striped flowers were a Victorian novelty too; just the sort of thing that you can imagine the Victorians liking. 'Striata Perfecta' was, I think, the first although it's no longer listed today. As with other garden plants, the names of notable breeders stand out in fuchsia history, and none was more distinguished than the Englishman James Lye. He raised wonderful varieties like 'Lye's Unique, 'Beauty of Swanley' and 'Amy Lye'.

But the story doesn't end there. The discovery of new fuchsias and their introduction to cultivation has continued to the present time, Professor Paul Berry of Wisconsin especially having been instrumental in finding many beautiful new species in South America.

And what of fuchsias' place in the overall scheme of botany? The genus belongs to the family Onagraceae, not one of gardening's greatest treasures. Apart from *Fuchsia*, it includes 23 relatively insignificant genera, among which *Oenothera* and *Gaura* and the willowherb genus *Epilobium* are among the more notable. In such company, there's no question that *Fuchsia* is the star.

The beautiful Brazilian species *Fuchsia coccinea* was among the first species to be brought to Europe

STRUCTURE AND PARTS OF A FLOWER

" Fuchsia flowers are so distinctive and so easily recognised that they immediately attract interest and attention. There is nothing else in the garden quite like them and while the flower of a Michaelmas daisy or a rose may be very beautiful in its way, there are countless other flowers of rather similar overall appearance. The distinctiveness of fuchsia flowers is further underlined by their foliage, which is somewhat uniform and, if not exactly dull, really does little more than set off the beauty of the blooms. With very few exceptions, no fuchsias would be grown for their foliage alone. "

As I have already indicated, fuchsia hybrids are so numerous and often have such complex breeding histories that they can't meaningfully be subdivided on the basis of their botanical origin or parentage. They are best categorised by their colour and it is on the basis of flower colour that this book is planned.

Much of the special appeal of fuchsia flowers depends, however, on the fact that individual parts of the flower may have quite separate and distinct colours. It's important, therefore, to understand how the flowers are made up and how the structure and appearance of each part is related to its function.

The principal features of a fuchsia flower are shown in the illustration. The flowers of most fuchsias, like the majority of those of other types of plant, are bisexual, containing both male, pollen-producing stamens and a female style with its stigma, on which pollen grains germinate as the prelude to fertilisation of the ovules in the ovary at the base. Some detailed accounts of fuchsia varieties include notes on the colour of the stamens and stigma but this information is seldom needed to differentiate one hybrid variety from another. It's worth noting, nonetheless, that one of the most unexpected and enchanting features to be found anywhere in the genus is the conspicuous bright blue pollen on the stamens of the New Zealand species in the Section Skinnera (page 32). In addition, the degree to which the stamens and stigma extend beyond the petals (are exerted from the flower) contributes much of the charm of individual species and varieties.

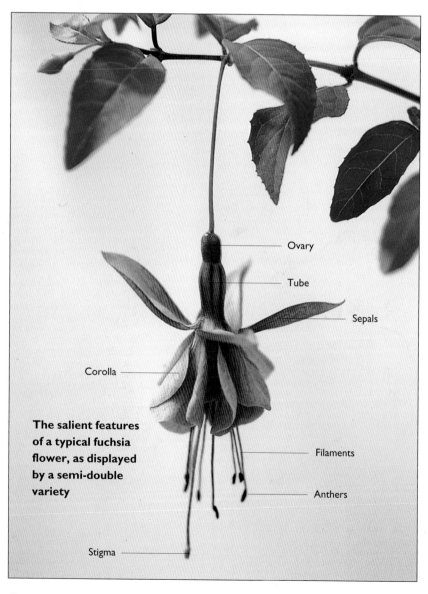

Ovary

Tube

Sepals

Corolla

The salient features of a typical fuchsia flower, as displayed by a semi-double variety

Filaments

Anthers

Stigma

More important than the sexual parts of the flower in description and classification are the colour and appearance of the sepals (which collectively form the calyx) and the petals (which collectively form the corolla). There are four sepals and four petals, the former flaring outwards at the top of a characteristic tube. In some fuchsias, especially some of the species and the beautiful varieties derived from *Fuchsia triphylla*, the tube may be extremely long and slender. The petals, which emerge at the mouth of the calyx tube, may be erect, spreading or reflexed (turned backwards). In a few groups, most notably the New Zealand species in the Section Skinnera, the petals are absent. Finally, and most importantly, there may be varying degrees of doubling of the flowers in which some or all of the stamens are converted to petals.

In the individual descriptions, I have given a general indication of flower size as small, medium or large. These are not intended as rigid divisions but approximate as follows (measurements are length from tip of the corolla to base of the tube):

Small – less than 2cm (¾in)
Medium – 2-3.5cm (¾-1½in)
Large – more than 3.5cm (1½in)

These lengths usually relate fairly closely to flower width: most large flowers are both long and broad, although flowers of the triphylla type and those of many species are distinctly narrow; where narrow flowers are proportionately very long, therefore, I have noted this.

Fuchsia 'Whiteknights Pearl', a single flowered variety

Fuchsia **'Deep Purple', a double flowered variety**

Fuchsia **'Thalia', a triphylla flowered variety**

PROPAGATION

" Fuchsias must be among the easiest of all garden plants to propagate. Many of the species may be raised very readily from seed, while almost all of the hybrids strike from cuttings with alacrity, so there is never an excuse for any gardeners, even the most inexperienced, having old, lax and woody specimens. The fact that they are, for vegetatively propagated plants, generally free from virus contamination (see page 22) also means that stock can be rejuvenated and perpetuated with ease. I have sometimes wondered if it is this ease of propagation that lies behind the constant stream of new fuchsia varieties. Because gardeners can so easily re-invigorate their own stock, they have little incentive to buy more plants of existing varieties; but might be interested in totally new ones. "

Fuchsia cutting ready for pushing into the tray of sand and compost

I now take fuchsia cuttings in the spring, primarily because it avoids the need to find warm growing space for young plants over winter. If the cuttings are taken at the most popular alternative time, in late summer, the plants must be potted up before the winter and, while they should have reached a reasonable size by the time that greenhouse shelter is needed, I find that their over-winter survival is much less certain than that of mature 'stock' plants.

I take softwood cuttings by removing new young growths from my over-wintered stock and trimming them to approximately 5cm (2in) in length, making the cut just below a node. I strip the leaves from the lower 2cm (1in) and dip the end in hormone rooting powder, taking care to knock off the excess. Most gardeners then strike the cuttings in sand or in a mixture of seedling compost and perlite. I prefer to use a layered technique that has served me well for many years. I half fill a seed tray with seedling compost and then top it up with a layer of sand. I push in the cuttings such that the base of each is at the sand and compost junction. I water them in the usual way and put a cover in place. The good aeration of the sand encourages rooting while the roots are immediately able to grow down into the nutrient containing medium.

As I explained above, however, fuchsia cuttings are so easy to strike that it is hard to fail; the only common problem to arise is if too many leaves are left on and the temperature is too low, when mould growth may set in.

Rooting will be more rapid (and mould growth less likely) if the cuttings are placed on a heated propagator.

Fuchsia cuttings form roots with alacrity and will soon be ready for potting on

They should then root within about two weeks, and the fact that rooting has occurred will be evident from the cuttings offering a slight springiness or resistance when gently pushed with the finger. If the shoots shows signs of elongation and new leaf growth, then rooting is certain. At this stage, the cuttings should be transplanted to individual 7cm (2¾in) diameter pots. Growth will be rapid and the plants will be ready for putting outside, after hardening off in the usual way, once the danger of frost has passed in late spring.

Although a few hybrid fuchsias are now obtainable as seed for raising yourself, I can see no merit in this. I find them inferior as flowering plants and the simplicity of propagating chosen forms from cuttings obviates any need for raising varieties from seed. Nonetheless, there is much pleasure and satisfaction to be derived from raising species from seed; and in some instances, this may be the only way of obtaining rare or unusual forms. My own preferred method is to obtain the seed as fresh as possible, washing it if necessary from the familiar ripe

purple fruit. The seeds are very small and should be sown sparingly on the surface of a seedling compost and then covered very thinly with sand, vermiculite or perlite. Cover the seed tray or pot and place it on a warm propagator. Seedling emergence is generally swift and uniform.

Prick on the seedlings in the usual way and the plants will flower within a few weeks in summer or if given winter warmth. Normally, however, I prefer to keep them until the following spring when I move them into their permanent pots.

PRUNING AND TRAINING

" *Fuchsias are shrubs; not bedding plants and not herbaceous perennials although they are sometimes grown as such. If they are allowed to, they can display a permanent framework or structure, just like any other shrub. But, also like any other shrub, the form that the plant adopts naturally may not be the most attractive or suitable for your garden. It is here that pruning and training come into their own.* "

Some varieties of fuchsias (and I have given this information in the individual plant entries) are self-branching and will form a neat plant and flower without any intervention on your part. If you want a flowering plant for the minimum of effort, those are the varieties to choose and around one-fifth of those in this book are self-branching types. Many varieties, including many of the most beautiful, however, will be straggly things and never achieve their real potential without a little help; it is both

simple and rewarding to provide this if you understand the principles.

Pinching

I refer on many occasions in the variety entries to the operation of 'pinching'. It is almost self-explanatory: using finger and thumb to pinch out the tips of the

With most varieties, pinching out is needed to produce the mass of flowers that make fuchsias so striking

RIGHT: The combination of one upright and one trailing variety can work well in a container

shoots to encourage branching further down, and hence a more compact, densely bushy plant. This is an operation that may be done to advantage even with plants being grown outdoors for one season only. But pinching to regulate the growth of individual shoots may also be part of a more ambitious process of shaping a fuchsia plant to a defined shape, much as fruit trees are shaped in the garden.

I have limited my descriptions here to the most common and straightforward forms, the bush, the standard and the pendent basket fuchsia. As you become more proficient, you may wish to experiment with some more tricky and advanced training methods such as pyramids, espaliers, fans or even pillars or cordons.

Training bush and shrub fuchsias

The following notes apply both to plants that naturally form a branching habit on a single stem (which fuchsia growers tend to call a bush) and those, most especially the species, that naturally form a branching habit on a number of separate stems, all arising from the same root (which they tend to call a shrub).

Feed and water the young plants, and insert canes for support as necessary (you will find it best to use unobtrusive green canes if possible). Once the leading shoot (or shoots if a shrub) has three pairs of leaves, pinch out the tip. Then pinch out the side-

shoots as they reach three pairs of leaves. This is called single-stopping. As further side-shoots arise from them in turn, these too can be pinched out at three pairs of leaves. This is called dou-

ble-stopping. You mustn't continue the process indefinitely, however, because most fuchsias (apart, notably from some of the species) flower at the shoot tips, so continual stopping will result in no flowers being produced. Bear in mind that, give or take more or less warmth and other factors, flowers will appear after 60 to 80 days from the time of stopping; double flowered varieties taking longer than singles.

A standard fuchsia can create a remarkably effective centre piece to many formal garden displays

Training standard fuchsias

Standard fuchsias are invariably the most admired exhibits at fuchsia shows but, because of their impressiveness, many gardeners imagine that they are difficult to produce and are creations for experts only. This is most definitely not so; it may be more ambitious than simple pinching but creating a standard

from a small rooted cutting is both easy and hugely satisfying.

From a batch of rooted cuttings in early spring, select a plant with a strong vertical shoot. If you have the opportunity, it is well worth searching among the cuttings for a plant that has three, not the normal two leaves at each node. This is a frequent mutation in fuchsias and some varieties are more prone to it than others. Because a side-shoot arises in each axil (the angle between the leaf and the stem), a three-leaved plant will inevitably produce more side-shoots and hence a denser, more bushy head. Varieties that I have described as suitable for bushes will make rounded standards; those that I have described as trailing will make weeping standards.

Use a small cane to support the chosen vertical shoot which, at all costs, mustn't be damaged. Then comes a continual process of training. Pinch out all side-shoots that arise on the stem anywhere below the top quarter; but leave the stem leaves in place until they fall naturally. On the top quarter of the stem, regularly pinch out the tips only of the side-shoots (as with a bush fuchsia) to encourage a well-filled head to form. As the plant fills its pot, move it on to a pot one size larger; to create a good standard, the plant mustn't suffer a check to growth. Stronger support canes will also be needed from time to time.

Once the plant has reached its desired height, pinch out the tip of the leading shoot and then continue to treat all of the shoots in the head in the same way, pinching out to maintain the shape. The 'desired height' can be whatever you choose but conventional

Care is needed in hanging baskets to choose other plants that blend with the very individual fuchsia shape and colours

sizes are approximately 25-45cm (10in-1½ft) for a quarter or 'table' standard, 45-75cm (1½-2½ft) for a half standard and 75cm-1.1m (1-3½ft) or more for a full standard. The procedures I have outlined will enable you easily to grow attractive, pleasing plants. Exhibitors seeking the perfection needed to win prizes at major shows will go to even greater trouble and care.

Hanging basket fuchsias

The hanging basket represents a particularly pleasing way of displaying fuchsias and, with the possible exception of the plant used in the centre, they should be of naturally lax or trailing habit. I discuss on page 18 the merits of mixing fuchsias with other plants as opposed to having baskets of fuchsias alone but the training is the same. With few exceptions (the ever-popular 'Swingtime' most notably) pendent fuchsias do not naturally branch a great deal. They tend to produce long lengths of internodes with

flowers at the tips. Just as with upright bush plants, pinching out these tips will encourage branching and yield more flowers. In general, however, I find it necessary to pinch out or stop pendent fuchsias rather more frequently than bush forms. Because of this, there is a good deal of merit in planting up the hanging basket in warm conditions as long as possible in advance of it being placed outside so the pinching can be completed earlier. It is here therefore that a heated greenhouse really comes into its own but you must still remember to harden off the hanging baskets before putting them outside.

15

CARE

" Not least among the pleasures of owning and growing fuchsias is that they are relatively undemanding plants. In this book, I have concentrated largely on their use as garden plants to give pleasure outdoors in the summer. A greenhouse is an almost essential requirement if more than a very few plants are to be kept successfully over winter; but it could also be used to advantage for those relatively few, more tender types that are best considered permanent indoor subjects. I have to admit, however, that during the summer months, almost my entire collection of fuchsias (including my considerable number of species) is somewhere outside in the garden. "

Apart from those used as bedding plants (page 20), most gardeners grow most of their fuchsias in containers, so the comments in the following two sections apply particularly to this method of growing.

Containers

Any type of container is suitable for growing fuchsias although as I have indicated on page 15, the hanging basket is especially appropriate for the trailing forms. The merits of different container styles are discussed in some detail in *Best Container Plants*.

Composts

Potting composts are divided broadly into soil-based and soil-less types. For many years, soil-less composts were synonymous with peat-based mixtures, and it is only since increasing awareness of the ecological importance of natural peatland habitats that alternatives have become available to gardeners. Those seen most commonly are based on coir (coconut fibre waste) but they have rather different properties from peat and I find them less satisfactory. I have largely reverted to carefully prepared proprietary soil-based composts, and

for British gardeners, this means those using the John Innes formula. All of my fuchsias are now grown in John Innes composts: cuttings and seedlings in the Seed formula, mature plants grown outdoors for a summer season in Potting Compost No. 2 and stock plants overwintered in the greenhouse in Potting Compost No. 1.

Most of the hardy fuchsia varieties tend to have smaller flowers; hardy double types are rare

Watering

Fuchsias are surprisingly tolerant of a lack of water by comparison with other woody container plants like azaleas. Nonetheless, they are not as drought tolerant as their common summer companions, pelargoniums, and in the summer garden, watering should be attended to at least twice each week.

Feeding

As with most plants, individual expert growers have their own, often strongly held views on the way that fuchsias should be fed. A change in the composition of the fertiliser at certain times during the season is commonly advocated. The gardener simply wanting a display of fuchsias for personal pleasure need not be concerned with this; a weekly feed with a proprietary soluble or liquid fertiliser with a relatively high potash content is perfectly adequate.

Over-wintering

Apart from the fuchsias that I have described as Fairly hardy, Moderately hardy or Hardy, some protection from frost must be given to the remainder in most temperate places if they are to be kept for the following year.

It is just possible for fuchsias to survive the winter in a state that I can best describe as hibernation: they are removed from the soil or compost in which they are growing, allowed to dry, their tops cut back severely, the roots dusted with fungicide and the plants then wrapped in bundles to be placed in a box in a frost-free shed or even buried in the garden. Gardeners with no alternative facilities will find that some of their plants will survive to be potted up in the spring, but it really should only be a method of last resort.

It is with more reliable methods of over-wintering that a greenhouse really comes into its own. Leaving aside for the moment formally trained plants, such as standards, there are essentially two ways of using the greenhouse to house normal 'garden' bush plants for the winter. If you take fuchsia cuttings in the autumn, you will require a considerable area of bench space for all your young plants.

If you take your cuttings in the spring, as I do, you will need to over-winter fairly large stock plants. In both cases, a minimum temperature of around 7°C (43°F) will be required. I simply select the plants that I intend to retain, cut down the top growth by around half in the autumn, remove them from their existing containers and pot them in John Innes No 1 compost in 20cm (8in) or smaller pots and place them in the greenhouse compartment from which my summer tomatoes have just been removed. They are watered no more than about once a month, and then only slightly, until the early spring. Then I begin giving a little more water as growth begins and, within a month, take cuttings to provide the season's plants. Trained plants of course are not cut down but are over wintered in exactly the same way, by reducing the watering and stopping feeding.

Plants hardy enough to survive outdoors in your area are best mulched around the crown with well-rotted compost or similar organic matter in the autumn. In areas where the top growth dies back even though the root-

stock survives, I find it advantageous to leave the dead shoots on over winter to provide added protection. They may then be cut back as new shoots arise from the base in spring. But do hang up sticky yellow cards to trap whitefly.

Fuchsias are often most successful when surrounded by foliage of other plants which help maintain a moist atmosphere

USING FUCHSIAS IN THE GARDEN

In my description of the special characteristics of fuchsias, I have mentioned their distinctly individual flower shape and also their limited overall range of colours, although it is a range within which almost every imaginable nuance and shade exists. This marked individuality of fuchsias makes them so valuable as garden plants; but it also means they must be placed carefully and their companions chosen with some thought. Colour considerations aside, fuchsias will thrive best in very slightly shaded, slightly moist conditions, yet it is amazing how plants in hanging baskets against a sunny south-facing wall manage to thrive too if given proper care.

Fuchsias as garden shrubs

Fuchsias can be grown in the open ground, either as permanent plants if they are sufficiently hardy, or as temporary subjects for the summer if they are not. For permanent plantings, they may be used much as any other small shrub but their distinctive colours are often especially well complemented by foliage plants (see *Best Foliage Shrubs* for my selection). But even foliage colour must be chosen with care. Unfortunate clashes have occurred in my own garden when I have used as companions deciduous shrubs with striking (especially yellow) autumn leaf colours.

Summer has passed peacefully but the shortening days of autumn have brought about effects that I had not expected. For the same reason, fuchsias such as 'Golden Marinka' that themselves have yellow leaves are particularly difficult to accommodate. I have found conifers to blend especially well with hardy fuchsias and here the individuality of the fuchsia works well alongside the more uniform texture and tonality of the conifer foliage (see *Best Conifers and Evergreens*). Remember, however, that most fuchsias hardy enough to

Only use a hardy fuchsia as a feature in areas where you are sure it won't be killed by an occasional frost

grow outside in European gardens are fairly small compared with many of the most attractive and popular shrubs, so place your fuchsias towards the front of the border.

Other than in mild areas where the above ground growth is not damaged by frost, fuchsias will inevitably be much less appealing in winter. The shoots will be killed by frost and will then be little more than bunches of brown twigs. I advocate leaving these dead shoots on over winter to provide protection for the crown of the plant, but no-one can pretend they are especially attractive at that time and so early spring flowering bulbs, planted close by, can help to enliven the spot.

Fuchsias as hedges

In mild areas, the fuchsia hedge can be thing of great delight; along the mild south-westerly coasts of Britain, hedges of naturalised *Fuchsia magellanica* are an accepted and very beautiful part of the landscape. Their small, more or less uniformly coloured flowers blend with native vegetation in a way that the more assertive bicoloured hybrid varieties never can. Fuchsia hedges may of course be planted deliberately in gardens in such districts where, in addition to *F. magellanica*, the varieties 'Riccartonii' and 'Mrs Popple' will also be successful. The plants should spaced 45cm (1½ft) apart and may be lightly

There isn't an ideal time to clip a fuchsia hedge; because of the long flowering period, some blooms will always be lost

clipped at any time during the growing season, as there is no period when they are out of flower. *F. magellanica* hedges will readily reach a height of 2m (6½ft) or more.

It is important to remember, however, that in planting a fuchsia hedge you will be planting something that will last fora long time. It is essential to plan exactly as for any other hedge therefore and prepare the planting position thoroughly with organic matter.

19

Fuchsias in summer bedding

Fuchsias may be used as bedding plants; trays of small plants are sold for this purpose. They are not ideal, however, for even the dwarf varieties will develop a loose, relatively tall and irregular form that soon becomes ungainly. The impossibility of effectively pinching the shoots when the plants are in a large bed compounds the problem. But fuchsias used as dot plants (taller, individual feature plants) among bedding can be most effective and standards can be especially dramatic. Do be aware of

the need to leave access to the plants for pinching out or dead-heading.

Fuchsias in containers

It is in containers that fuchsias really come in to their own in the garden. Like all container plants, they can be placed exactly where they are needed; and then moved as the season progresses. I prefer to use them as individual specimens as I feel their impact is greater then but it is worth adding one other consideration. Fuchsias need some moisture in the air; and a mixed planting does at least tend to

It is the cascading form of the trailing or pendant fuchsias that appeal to many gardeners

offer that because moisture is liberated by the foliage of other surrounding plants. Fuchsias that are to be grown in full sun are, therefore, generally better in a mixture.

In containers, standard plants once again can be highly effective but, as with standard roses, tend to be better in relatively formal gardens than in softer, semi-natural plantings. A carefully stopped fuchsia bush or shrub, clothed from top to bottom with flowers can also be utterly arresting; so much so in truth that it can upstage everything else. I am particularly fond of using trailing varieties as individual specimens in pots atop a pedestal from which the blooms cascade down.

Fuchsias are often used in window boxes but are seldom at their most effective there because the window box, by virtue of its shape and position, cannot offer ideal growing conditions either for upright bush plants or for trailing forms. The limited size of the window box itself will restrict you either to a planting of the rather few dwarf varieties or to a summer-long commitment to pinching and stopping.

The hanging basket is considered by many gardeners to be the ideal container for fuchsia growing, partly because it allows trailing varieties to be shown off so well. There's no denying that either planted with several specimens of a single fuchsia variety or with a mixture of upright and trailing bedding plants, a well-prepared and carefully maintained hanging basket can turn heads. Although hanging baskets are usually seen adorning a house wall, remember that an even more arresting feature can be created by using a free-standing support on which three or more baskets are suspended.

Very commonly I see baskets in which up to 10 different types of plant (fuchsias among them) have been used, quite commonly with some thought having been given to their relative growth rates and habits; but none at all to the colour. If a 'riot of colour' is what appeals to you, then that is what you should have, but just take a look at some carefully colour co-ordinated baskets (most big garden shows have

hanging baskets classes) to realise what beauty can be achieved; and how fuchsias, individual as they are, can play their part in that.

Fuchsias as house plants

I am often asked about the suitability of fuchsias as house-plants. After all, if they require greenhouse protection in the winter, could they not be put to good purpose in beautifying our homes? The answer, by and large, is no. In times past, fuchsias were used considerably indoors (and of course the 'table standard' was created originally to form a dining table centre-piece). But this was before the advent of central heating dried the air in our homes and created conditions that are not to their liking, and that are more than likely to encourage the appearance of red spider mite.

ABOVE: My advice is to resist using fuchsias as house plants

BELOW: I still think that a single variety makes the greatest impact in a container

PESTS, DISEASES AND DISORDERS

❝ Outdoors, I find fuchsias relatively pest and disease free and it is rare that my summer display is significantly affected. Indoors, it is rather a different matter and plants being kept in growth over winter or permanently in a green-house will almost inevitably require some significant attention, espe-cially from the most important pests, red spider mite and the glasshouse whitefly. The most important disease of fuchsias in most gardens is the grey mould, Botrytis, which thrives in the close, confined and damp atmosphere among the foliage. Fortunately and rather surprisingly for vegeta-tively propagated plants, fuchsias are not prone to virus attack and cuttings may be taken for genera-tions without deterioration. ❞

Fuchsia rust is a disease that has increased in importance in recent years

The accompanying chart should enable you to identify almost all pests and diseases that you are likely to encounter on fuchsias in European gardens.

Details of different types of fungicide and insecticide and also more informa-tion on biological control of pests can be found in *Best Garden Doctor*.

Symptoms	Probable cause	Treatment
Flowers (especially white varieties), leaves and/or buds rotten with fluffy grey mould growth present	Grey mould (Botrytis)	Remove and destroy affected parts and spray plants with systemic fungicide. Try to improve ventilation and reduce humidity
Flowers and/or buds fail to form or drop prematurely	Dry air	Use mist or other means to maintain a damp and 'buoyant' atmosphere
Leaves and stems infested by green, yellow or pink wingless and winged insects; foliage sticky and sooty	Aphids	Use proprietary insecticide spray
Leaves discoloured, yellowing, bronzing and dying; many small mites on undersides of leaves	Red spider mite	Use mist or other means to maintain a damp and 'buoyant' atmosphere. Chemical sprays are of very limited value
Leaves mottled on surface but no mites present	Leafhoppers	The insects are too erratic in their occurrence to justify control measures

Leaves variously discoloured in a diffuse manner with few discrete spots	Nutrient deficiency	Take care to use balanced and appropriate fertiliser (page 16)
Leaves wilt; stem interior with brown or black streaks	Wilt disease	Destroy affected plants and, if in pots, dispose of compost
Leaves with pale yellow patches and tiny orange pustules beneath	Fuchsia rust	Pull off and destroy affected leaves. No rust fungicides are effective and safe enough to use on fuchsias which are easily damaged by chemicals
Leaves with small tattered holes, especially at tips of young shoots	Capsid bugs	The insects are too erratic in their occurrence to justify control measures
Leaves with small winged insects and yellow scales on undersides, foliage sticky and sooty	Whitefly	Use Encarsia biological control in greenhouses
Plants (especially young plants and cuttings) with irregular holes and pieces eaten out of leaves, flowers, stems or buds; slime trails present on or near plants	Slugs and snails	Use proprietary slug baits, taking care to protect them from pets and wild life
Plants with irregular holes and pieces eaten out of leaves, buds and flowers; no slime trails present; very large caterpillars may be present	Caterpillars; the very large (8cm/3¼in) long caterpillars are the larvae of elephant hawk moths	Elephant hawk moth caterpillars should be placed on alternative food plants such as willowherb. Use proprietary biological or chemical spray for other caterpillar species
Plants with many small dark flies running over surface of soil or potting medium; white, legless larvae with dark heads sometimes present among roots and at bases of stems	Fungus gnats	Take care not to under or over-water plants; if the problem persists, water spray strength proprietary insecticide on to compost
Plants with minute, wingless insects jumping from surface of potting compost	Springtails	Take care not to over-water and allow the compost to become very acidic
Plants with roots eaten by C-shaped legless grubs, especially in pots	Vine weevil larvae	Take cuttings and then destroy affected plants and compost; use nematode-based biological control
Roots rotten; plants generally unhealthy	Root and foot rot	Destroy plants and ensure that new plants are in well-drained, fresh compost

SECTION QUELUSIA

The Quelusia fuchsias are characterised by long stamens, exerted from the flower and by the tube generally being no longer than the sepals. They were among the earliest species to reach Europe from their homelands in Argentina, Brazil and Chile. This is a hugely important group because of the large number of relatively hardy types that it embraces and also because, among them, is Fuchsia magellanica, the most significant of all hardy species. The plants in this group should form the core of any collection of hardy species.

Fuchsia alpestris (syn. *F. regia* var. *alpestris*)

ORIGIN: First found in the Serra dos Orgoas mountains in the south-east of Brazil and introduced to Britain in 1842.
COROLLA COLOUR: Purple.
TUBE COLOUR: Deep red.
SEPAL COLOUR: Red.
FLOWER FORM: Single.
FLOWER SIZE: Small.
HARDINESS: Barely hardy.

Fuchsia coccinea

PLANT HABIT/GARDEN USES

A shrubby plant that can reach 1.5-6m (5-20ft) in favourable conditions. In a very sheltered position, train it to climb up a warm wall or allow it to spread over the ground. In colder areas, grow it in containers so it may be overwintered in a greenhouse.

NOTABLE FEATURES

An unusual outdoor fuchsia for a sheltered spot; the young leaves have 'autumnal' tints.

Fuchsia coccinea

ORIGIN: The history of this plant is both confused and interesting. It was long believed to be a Chilean species, because of an erroneous identification of a plant growing at Kew in 1789, which had been brought there from Lisbon by one Captain Firth and evidently collected in South America the previous year. In reality, the Kew plant had been confused with *Fuchsia magellanica*, which this species does resemble.

It was many years before Sir Joseph Hooker rightly realised that the Kew specimen was different and almost certainly a Brazilian species, later named *F. coccinea*. Even now, the name is still sometimes confusingly used as a synonym for at least one form of *F. magellanica*.

F. coccinea had almost died out in cultivation when two plants were found in the greenhouses of the Oxford Botanic Garden in 1867 and rescued. Since then it has been used considerably in breeding but it seems to have become rare in its native habitat, sadly an all too common occurence with many South American plants.

COROLLA COLOUR: Purple
TUBE COLOUR: Scarlet.
SEPAL COLOUR: Red.
FLOWER FORM: Single.
FLOWER SIZE: Small.
HARDINESS: Barely hardy.

Other recommended species

The following are all Tender to Barely hardy.

F. brevilobis, Brazil, introduced by Berry in 1989, corolla purple, tubular, sepals and tube red, tube elongated and 'embracing' the petals, small flowers, mid-green elongated foliage, arching lax habit to 1m (3ft).

F. gehrigeri, Western Venezuela in cloud forest at 2,200 to 3,100m, corolla scarlet, tube and sepals red, small to medium flowers produced in the leaf-axils and at the ends of stalks, pear-shaped dark purple fruit, an upright shrub with flexible branches that grows like a climber and which can reach 2-5m (6½-16ft), at least in its native habitat. *F. gehrigeri* is sometimes placed in the Section Fuchsia.

F. glaziovana, Brazil, found by Berry in the 1980s in cloud forest north-west of Rio de Janeiro, purple corolla, deep pink tube and sepals, single flowers, shrub-like growth reaching 4m (13ft) in its native habitat.

F. hatsbachii, Brazil, introduced by Berry in 1989, corolla violet, sepals and tube red, small axillary flowers, dark green foliage, straggling wiry habit; mine attains about 1m (3ft) each year after I cut it back almost to the base. These species provide graphic evidence that even now, there are many wild plants yet to be discovered.

PLANT HABIT/GARDEN USES

Upright, bushy growth reaching 1m (3ft) although occasionally producing long, slender shoots up to 3m (10ft) in length. Best grown in a large container for overwintering in a greenhouse.

NOTABLE FEATURES

One of the first fuchsias to be sold as a garden plant in the UK and because nurserymen discovered that it crosses with ease, a parent of many of the early fuchsia hybrids.

Fuchsia glaziovana

SECTION QUELUSIA

Fuchsia magellanica

ORIGIN: A native of southern Chile and bordering areas of Argentina, south to Tierra del Fuego. Its habitat is in moist regions along streams and in marshy places; it is found typically in the mountain rain forests near the Strait of Magellan. It occurs naturally at altitudes of up to 3,000m so is hardy enough for the winters in many parts of Europe and, interestingly, often occurs in the wild with a plant that I have long considered one of the most desirable of all evergreen shrubs, *Berberis darwinii*, although that species is less moisture-demanding. *Fuchsia magellanica* is often said to have been introduced to Europe by Lamarck in 1768 but this almost certainly stems from confusion with *F. coccinea* (see page 25) and it seems probable that it didn't really arrive until around 1823. Forms of it have become rather extensively naturalised along the west coast of Britain and in many other parts of the world. It is the only *Fuchsia* species listed among the British Flora.

COROLLA COLOUR: Bright purple when the blooms open but then fades.

TUBE COLOUR: Deep red.

SEPAL COLOUR: Deep red.

FLOWER FORM: Single

FLOWER SIZE: Small to medium.

HARDINESS: Hardy.

PLANT HABIT/GARDEN USES

In mild, and especially coastal areas, the shrubby growth up to 3.5m (11ft) is not cut back by frost so these plants can be used very successfully and attractively as hedging. In colder areas, they may be grown as specimen shrubby perennials in borders or courtyards. When grown as a hedge, they should be clipped lightly in summer but because of the very long flowering period of fuchsias, some loss of blooms is inevitable.

NOTABLE FEATURES

The magellanicas are the hardiest of all fuchsias, thriving in sun or moist shade, *F. magellanica* making a reliable versatile hardy shrub for late summer colour.

Fuchsia magellanica

Fuchsia magellanica 'Versicolor'

Recommended forms
The following are all Hardy.

The following three very desirable forms are variants of the natural variety *gracilis* which was introduced from Chile in 1822 by the botanist and explorer Alexander Cruckshanks who sent seed to the London collector Francis Place. As is evident therefore, it does come true from seed. The variety is characterised by slender arching branches, often rather downy to the touch.

F. magellanica var. *gracilis* 'Aurea', corolla purple, sepals and tube red, gold-yellow foliage, small single flowers, a hardy garden shrub but not as vigorous as the green-leaved variety and attaining about 2m (6½ft).

F. magellanica var. *gracilis* 'Variegata' (AGM), grown for its foliage which is green with white margins and spots, red and purple-blue flowers, a small shrub up to 60cm (2ft), less hardy than the green-leaved variety as is usual with variegated plants.

F. magellanica var. *gracilis* 'Tricolor', similar to 'Variegata' but with more striking foliage displaying three colours, a grey-green, pink and yellow. The intensity of the colours is less in shade and the low growing habit makes it an ideal companion for summer bedding plants.

F. magellanica 'Versicolor' (syn. *F.* 'Versicolor') (AGM), silver grey-green foliage with red-pink flush when young and bright red variegated regions, small, single red and purple flowers.

F. magellanica var. *gracilis* 'Aurea'

SECTION FUCHSIA

> ❝ *The Section Fuchsia is the largest in the genus with far and away the greatest number of species. It is graced with the name Fuchsia because it contains* Fuchsia triphylla *which is not only a very important plant horticulturally but is also the type species (the first species to be described and that upon which the description of the entire genus* Fuchsia *is founded). All of the fuchsias in this section have very short sepals and a very long tube which gives them, for me and many other gardeners, a uniquely attractive appeal. The flowers are always some shade of red, never blue or purple although occasionally enlivened with green. Their natural distribution lies in Haiti and the Dominican Republic (the old island of Hispaniola) in the northern Caribbean through Central America and Venezuela, and down the Andes of Colombia, Ecuador, Bolivia and Peru into northern Chile.* ❞

Fuchsia corymbiflora (syn. *F. dependens*)

ORIGIN: Peru, introduced around 1877.
COROLLA COLOUR: Dark scarlet.
TUBE COLOUR: Scarlet.
SEPAL COLOUR: Scarlet.
FLOWER FORM: Single.
FLOWER SIZE: Small but long.
HARDINESS: Barely hardy.

PLANT HABIT/GARDEN USES

A beautiful upright shrubby plant reaching 1-4m (3-13ft) although in gardens, it is best restricted by annual pruning. I grow it in a container and cut the top growth back to about 30cm (1ft) each year. It then reaches about 1.5m (5ft) during the season.

NOTABLE FEATURES

Vine-like growth (given space) with the flowers forming large, dense terminal clusters and with particularly large, elongated leaves. An extremely easy plant to raise from seed.

Fuchsia corymbiflora

Fuchsia boliviana

ORIGIN: Named after Bolivia where it was originally collected, but also found in Argentina and Peru. It is now naturalised in Colombia and Venezuela also. Certainly in cultivation by 1876.
COROLLA COLOUR: Scarlet.
TUBE COLOUR: Scarlet to dark red.
SEPAL COLOUR: Scarlet to dark red.
FLOWER FORM: Single.
FLOWER SIZE: Small but long (5cm/2in).
HARDINESS: Barely hardy.

PLANT HABIT/GARDEN USES

Upright shrub reaching 1.2-1.8m (4-5¾ft) with flowers in pendulous terminal racemes and very like *F. corymbiflora* in overall form and appearance. Its profuse flowers, large 20 x 3cm (8 x 1¼in) velvety leaves with red veins and berries that turn from pale green to black-purple make it a splendid specimen. In a heated conservatory it will bloom all year round. Alternatively, it can be overwintered in frost-free conditions and used as a summer bedding plant or grown as I grow it, as a summer specimen in a large container.

NOTABLE FEATURES

One of the racemose fuchsias that flower profusely and for a long period. An exotic-looking, tender and extremely beautiful plant that can be distinguished from *F. corymbiflora* by its reflexed sepals.

Fuchsia boliviana var. *alba* (syn. *F. b.* 'Alba', *F. b.* var. *luxurians*, *F. corymbiflora alba*)

ORIGIN: This is a variant that was found in the wild in its native Bolivia. A French gardener named Courcelles is thought to have introduced it to Europe in 1850.
COROLLA COLOUR: Deep red.
TUBE COLOUR: White.
SEPAL COLOUR: Deep red.
FLOWER FORM: Single.
FLOWER SIZE: Small but long (5cm/2in).
HARDINESS: Tender.

PLANT HABIT/GARDEN USES

As the normal species.

Fuchsia boliviana

NOTABLE FEATURES

Similar to *F. boliviana* but has a white tube and larger velvet leaves with no red veining.

Fuchsia loxensis

Other recommended species
The following are all Tender to Barely hardy.

F. ampliata (syn. *F. canescens*), introduced from Ecuador in 1877, corolla orange-red, tube and sepals scarlet to orange-red, red-purple veins on foliage, small flowers, shrubby upright growth to 3m (10ft).
F. andrei, from Ecuador and Peru, corolla orange-red, tube and sepals orange-red to scarlet, small flowers in racemes, tender, shrubby growth up to 4m (13ft) in its native habitat; in temperate climates best grown in containers in a greenhouse or conservatory, there is a characteristic waxy texture to the flowers and leaves.
F. austromontana (syn. *F. serratifolia*), Bolivia and Peru, introduced in 1844,

deep red corolla, scarlet tube and sepals, small, axillary flowers, upright reddish growth to 4m (13ft).
F. cinerea, Ecuador and Colombia, red-orange corolla, orange tube, orange sepals with green tips, silvery hairy leaves with red-brown veins, small but 2.5cm (1in) long flowers that are axillary and pendent, upright shrubby growth to 5m (16ft) in its native habitat but in Britain about 60cm (2ft).
F. decussata, Peru, introduced by William Lobb for the Veitch Nursery in 1843-4, scarlet to red-orange corolla, red tube, red sepals with green tips, small axillary flowers but produced profusely over a long period, upright climber to 3m (10ft) in its native habitat.
F. denticulata (syn. *F. serratifolia*), Peru and Bolivia, introduced by William

Lobb with *F. decussata*, orange or scarlet corolla (there is some variation between specimens), light red tube, red sepals with green-white tips, small but long single axillary flowers borne profusely, best grown in containers or in a greenhouse border, upright shrubby growth to 4m (13ft).
F. hartwegii, Colombia, red corolla, red-orange tube and sepals, red veins on foliage, small flowers mostly in racemes, an upright climbing shrub to 4m (13ft).
F. loxensis, Ecuador, scarlet-orange corolla, dull red tube and sepals, shiny light green leaves with red veins, axillary flowers 2.5cm (1in) long, grows to a mound 60cm (2ft) high without the need for pinching and training and can be used successfully in hanging baskets.

Fuchsia pallescens

ORIGIN: Ecuador and Colombia.
COROLLA COLOUR: Dark red to maroon.
TUBE COLOUR: Pink to pale red.
SEPAL COLOUR: Pink to pale red.
FLOWER FORM: Single.
FLOWER SIZE: Small.
HARDINESS: Tender to Barely hardy.

PLANT HABIT/GARDEN USES

Low-growing shrub with shiny flowers and velvety, dark green hairy leaves.

NOTABLE FEATURES

The mass of tiny flowers seen against the dark green foliage can be very dramatic if the plant is kept neat and compact.

Fuchsia sanctae-rosae

Fuchsia sanctae-rosae (syn. *F. boliviana*)

ORIGIN: Named by Kuntze in 1892, this species is native to Bolivia and Peru.
COROLLA COLOUR: Pale orange-red.
TUBE COLOUR: Orange-red.
SEPAL COLOUR: Pale orange-red.
FLOWER FORM: Single.
FLOWER SIZE: Small.
HARDINESS: Tender.

PLANT HABIT/GARDEN USES

Shrubby upright habit reaching to 3m (10ft) in its native habitat with red-purple stems. Hairy glossy green leaves. Shiny flowers grow singly in the leaf axils. Needs careful cultivation as it tends to lose its leaves if watering and feeding is erratic.

NOTABLE FEATURES

Striking tree-like growth with axillary flowers.

Fuchsia triphylla

ORIGIN: A native of Hispaniola (Haiti and the Dominican Republic), this hugely important and striking plant was first discovered around 1695 by the French explorer Charles Plumier in the foothills around Santo Domingo but the plants were lost. Philip Miller of the Chelsea Physic Garden raised plants from seed around 1700 but these too were lost. Seed was probably not collected again until 1873 by Thomas Hogg and plants from this collection were raised at the New York Botanic Garden. Some found their way to England and were distributed by Henderson & Son of St John's Wood, London as *F. racemosa*.
COROLLA COLOUR: Orange to coral red.
TUBE COLOUR: Orange-red to coral red.
SEPAL COLOUR: Orange-red to coral red
FLOWER FORM: Triphylla.
FLOWER SIZE: Small but long tubes (3cm/1¼in).
HARDINESS: Tender to Barely hardy.

PLANT HABIT/GARDEN USES

A low-growing shrub reaching about 45cm (1½ft) with red hairy young growth. The foliage has a wonderful velvet texture and is dark green with a purple flush and red veins.

NOTABLE FEATURES

The first *Fuchsia* species to be

described, it has been used extensively in breeding to give rise to the popular long-tubed 'triphylla hybrids' (direct descendants); the similar 'triphylla types' are derived from closely related plants.

Fuchsia triphylla

Fuchsia lycioides

Other recommended species
The following are all Tender to Barely hardy.

F. lycioides (syn. *F. rosea*), Chile, introduced in 1807, corolla rose-pink, tube pale-pink, sepals pale-pink, small flowers, axillary flowering along rigid stems; fleshy leaves have helped the plant survive the dry and extreme conditions of the Atacama desert in Chile; when the leaves are shed small spines are formed, upright shrubby growth to 3m (10ft). There are very few other *Fuchsia* species that are so tolerant of dry conditions, in gardens as well as deserts.

F. macrophylla, Peru, corolla bright scarlet, tube red, sepals red with green tips, dark green foliage with red veins, small flowers but large leaves up to 15cm (6in) long, upright shrub with red-purple tinge to young growth.

F. magdalenae, Colombia, in cloud forest at 2,000 to 3,500m, corolla orange-red, tube bright orange-red with purple at the base, sepals bright orange-red with green tips, purple fruits and purple tinge to young growth, medium-sized flowers with long tube up to 6cm (2¼in) and medium to large leaves slightly serrated, shrubby growth from 2-5m (6½-16ft) in its native habitat.

F. nigricans, Venezuela, Colombia, corolla purple, tube and sepals light red, small flowers but long tube, upright shrubby plant up to 3m (10ft).

F. petiolaris, Venezuela and Colombia, corolla bright red-pink, tube shiny rose, sepals shiny pale pink with green tips, foliage has fine hairs, small to medium-sized flowers with long tube and sepals, upright shrub or climber up to 2m (6½ft) in its native habitat.

F. putumayensis, Ecuador and Colombia, corolla orange-red, tube and sepals orange-red to coral red, small but long flowers, medium to large leaves with hairs on upper surface, shrubby growth to 3m (10ft) in its native habitat.

F. simplicicaulis, Peru, corolla red, tube and sepals pale red-pink, small flowers with long tube and sepals, flowers borne in racemes, medium to large elongated leaves, rather downy beneath, climber reaching 5m (16ft) in its native habitat but 2m (6½ft) in cultivation.

F. vargarsiana, corolla red, tube red, sepals red with green tips, medium to large leaves of shiny dark green, small flowers in terminal racemes, upright shrub 1.5-2m (5-6½ft), in its native habitat.

F. venusta, Colombia and Venezuela, corolla red-orange to orange, tube shiny orange red, sepals orange-red with green tips, small to medium flowers have a long tube and narrow petals and sepals which give a spidery effect, axillary flowering, medium to large leaves of glossy dark green, blue-purple stems, climbs to 3m (10ft) in its native habitat or about 1.5m (5ft) in cultivation.

F. wurdackii, Peru, introduced in 1962, corolla red, tube and sepals coral red, small to medium flowers in terminal racemes, medium to large foliage and young growth covered in fine hairs, upright shrub to 1.5m (5ft) in its native habitat.

SECTION SKINNERA

" This group contains the fuchsias that are, in so many ways, the anomalies of the genus. There are only four species but they include the largest fuchsia and one of the smallest. They are geographically isolated in Tahiti and New Zealand, their flowers are variable and are beautifully if unexpectedly coloured yellow, brown, orange or very dark purple while the pollen is dramatically blue. They might not be typical fuchsias but they are quite fantastic plants. "

Fuchsia perscandens

ORIGIN: New Zealand.
COROLLA COLOUR: Dark purple.
TUBE COLOUR: Yellow-green.
SEPAL COLOUR: Purple-brown.
FLOWER FORM: Single.
FLOWER SIZE: Small.
HARDINESS: Barely hardy.

PLANT HABIT/GARDEN USES

A scrambling shrub with small elongated leaves with whitish undersides. It isn't striking enough on its own but useful in a group.

NOTABLE FEATURES

The flowers are interesting rather than dramatic and it is a species that I find tends to become woody and lax unless cut back annually. It also tends to lose its leaves from the the lower parts of its branches.

Fuchsia procumbens **in flower**

Fuchsia procumbens (AGM)

ORIGIN: New Zealand, introduced around 1854 after being discovered on North Island in 1834 by the English plant collector Allan Cunningham. He collected extensively in South America, Australia and New Zealand and died in Sydney, two years after succeeding his brother there as Superintendent of the Botanic Gardens.
COROLLA COLOUR: No corolla.
TUBE COLOUR: Yellow-orange with purple-red at the base.
SEPAL COLOUR: Brown.
FLOWER FORM: Single.
FLOWER SIZE: Small.
HARDINESS: Barely hardy to Fairly hardy.

PLANT HABIT/GARDEN USES

A trailing plant with thin wiry stems up to 1m (3ft) long and with very small rounded leaves. The flowers stand upright and their stamens with blue pollen are very conspicuous. An interesting feature is the abnormally large pink-purple fruit, like miniature plums; they are edible and were eaten by the Maoris. Use it as a creeping plant on a sunny rock garden or grow it in a tall container and let the branches cascade over the sides; it joins other *Fuchsia* species in my garden on top of a wooden rain butt in the damp and sheltered fern garden where it survives for all except the coldest months of the year. In its native habitat, it grows on rocky, coastal sites.

NOTABLE FEATURES:

Prostrate species only 5cm (2in) high, the only cultivated species with a yellow tube. This really is an absolutely essential component of any collection of *Fuchsia* species and is also very easy to grow. Although it is certainly not a typical member of the genus, I think it would probably feature on a short list of my favourites.

Other recommended species
The following are all Barely hardy.

F. x colensoi, Tahiti and New Zealand, probably a naturally occurring hybrid with *F. excorticata* as one parent, a very variable plant, corolla purple, tube red-purple, sepals green to red, small leaves with more or less white undersides, a slightly untidy shrubby habit with long trailing branches.

F. excorticata, New Zealand, introduced around 1820 and grown in James Colvill's famous nursery in the King's Road, Chelsea, dark purple corolla with blue anthers and yellow stigma, green tube and sepals that later become red-purple, small inconspicuous pendulous flowers, medium-sized leaves with white undersides are the main feature, the bark is light brown and papery. In its native New Zealand it grows into a 10m (33ft) tall tree (probably the largest of all fuchsias) and it makes a large bush in mild areas of Britain; I grow it in a container and cut it back annually but however it is grown, I find it a shy flowerer in cultivation.

Fuchsia procumbens in fruit

MISCELLANEOUS SPECIES

“ *The remaining six sections of the genus contain a wide range of species from which I have selected a few Central American types that are particularly appealing and are reasonably readily obtainable from European nurseries. Fuchsia arborescens is one of two Central American species that comprise the Section Schufa, while F. encliandra and F. microphylla are two of a small group in the Central American Section Encliandra which have given rise to a number of cultivated hybrids with character-istically tiny, delicate, almost fern-like leaves and small, individually borne flowers. F. splendens is one of three, fairly vigorous, shrubby species in the Section Ellobium.* ”

Fuchsia arborescens (syn. *F. arborea*)

ORIGIN: Mexico, introduced in 1824.
COROLLA COLOUR: Lavender.
TUBE COLOUR: Rose.
SEPAL COLOUR: Rose.
FLOWER FORM: Single.
FLOWER SIZE: Very small but very numerous flowers borne in large panicles.
HARDINESS: Tender to Barely hardy.

PLANT HABIT/GARDEN USES

In its native habitat it forms a tree 6-8m (20-25ft) high, whereas in Britain, it is a large erect bush of up to 3m (10ft).

Often the flowers and sloe-like fruits occur on the plant at the same time. It has shiny medium-large leaves with red veins.

NOTABLE FEATURES

Unusual flowers, it appears superficially more like a lilac than a fuchsia (an earlier and now obsolete name was F. syringaeflora), so small are the individual flowers. It usually blooms during the winter so is best grown as a warm conservatory or greenhouse plant where it can be a very striking addition to the range of winter-flowering shrubs. Strangely, for one of the largest species of *Fuchsia*, this plant has some of the smallest flowers.

Fuchsia arborescens

Fuchsia encliandra ssp. encliandra

ORIGIN: Mountains of Mexico.
COROLLA COLOUR: Red.
TUBE COLOUR: Red.
SEPAL COLOUR: Red.
FLOWER FORM: Single.
FLOWER SIZE: Very small.
HARDINESS: Tender.

PLANT HABIT/GARDEN USES

Although the leaves and flowers are very small, the plant itself is vigorous with long arching branches.

NOTABLE FEATURES

A distinctive, untypical fuchsia appearance.

Fuchsia splendens

Fuchsia microphylla

Other recommended species
The following are Barely hardy.

F. splendens (syn. *F. cordifolia*) (AGM), Mexico and Costa Rica, introduced in 1832, corolla orange, rose tube, sepals orange-red with green tips, small but elongated axillary flowers with yellow anthers, heart-shaped downy leaves of grey-green with red stems, shrubby upright growth to 2.5m (8ft) in its native habitat; in Britain, a winter-flowering plant about 50cm (1¾ft) tall for a warm greenhouse or conservatory. It is a plant that I think I have in my own collection; an unidentified Mexican species given to me seems to fit the description very closely. If so, then it is one I commend but don't be disappointed at the lack of summer flowers. Worth waiting for in winter, although you must not disturb the plant or it will drop them in alarm.

F. microphylla, Central America, introduced in 1828, corolla rose, tube and sepals red, very small 6mm (¼in) flowers like tiny cigars, very small 13mm (½in) leaves, bushy habit and year-round flowering ability make it suitable for summer courtyards or conservatories although it will survive in a sheltered border in mild areas, size ranges from 50cm (1¾ft) upwards in cultivation but up to 5m (16ft) in its native habitat.

VARIETIES WITH MAINLY WHITE PETALS

White flowers, even in the wild, are no rarity. The absence of pigmentation, so giving rise to white, occurs as a pretty common mutation in many, probably most groups of plants. Sometimes the condition stabilises to the extent of white flowers becoming so constant a characteristic that the form is justified in being called a new species. In other cases, it is an occasional event, and so the white-flowered plant becomes a variety. When the white flowers arise in cultivation, the form is strictly called not a variety but a cultivar and these white-flowered cultivars are so frequent that the name 'Alba' is the commonest in all of horticulture. So it is with fuchsias: a number of white-flowered species occur in the wild and white-petalled variants have clearly arisen many times and been used in breeding programmes. The first double white-petalled variety was probably the patriotically named 'Queen Victoria' around 1850. But while white petals, either with coloured sepals and tube or as part of entirely white flowers, had long been known, fuchsias that offered the reverse, a combination of white sepals and tube with coloured petals, were unknown until 'Venus Victrix' arose in 1840 (see page 93).

Fuchsia 'Bobby Shaftoe'

ORIGIN: Ryle, UK 1970.
COROLLA COLOUR: White, flushed with palest pink with pink veins.
TUBE COLOUR: Clear frosty white with pale pink flush.
SEPAL COLOUR: White, pink undersides with lemon-green tips.
FLOWER FORM: Semi-double.
FLOWER SIZE: Medium.
HARDINESS: Tender to Barely hardy.

PLANT HABIT/GARDEN USES

Well-branched upright bush with small dark green foliage. Prolific flowers on a short-jointed plant.

NOTABLE FEATURES

I always appreciate the contrast of the two whites in this variety: the slightly cream-white of the petals with the sharper, icy white of the tube. It's too easy for gardeners to say that all whites are the same.

Fuchsia 'Devonshire Dumpling'

Fuchsia 'Devonshire Dumpling'

ORIGIN: Hilton, UK 1981.
COROLLA COLOUR: White, flushed with pink.
TUBE COLOUR: White.
SEPAL COLOUR: Pale pink with green tips.
FLOWER FORM: Double.
FLOWER SIZE: Large.
HARDINESS: Tender to Barely hardy.

PLANT HABIT/GARDEN USES

Strong grower with free-branching habit, large blooms. Bush, standard or in large hanging basket.

NOTABLE FEATURES

One of the best varieties for habit and continuous production of large numbers of flowers. I have grown it for many years in my largest hanging basket.

Fuchsia 'Torvill and Dean'

ORIGIN: Pacey, UK 1985.
COROLLA COLOUR: White flushed with pink.
TUBE COLOUR: Pink.
SEPAL COLOUR: Pink.
FLOWER FORM: Double.
FLOWER SIZE: Large.
HARDINESS: Tender to Barely hardy.

PLANT HABIT/GARDEN USES

Upright bushy habit with short joints, free flowering. This plant is best grown in containers as a bush or small standard. The blooms are very similar to those of 'Cotton Candy', although I don't know if they share parentage.

NOTABLE FEATURES

This is one of those varieties that has, I suspect, achieved its present position due more to the popularity of the inspirations for its name than any particular horticultural merits.

Fuchsia **'Baby Bright'**

Fuchsia **'Torvill and Dean'**

Other recommended varieties

The following are Tender to Barely hardy unless otherwise stated.

F. 'Annabel' (AGM), Ryle, UK 1977, ['Ingram Maid' x 'Nancy Lou'], pure white flowers, only tinged with pink when grown in full sun, profuse double flowers, pale green foliage, upright growth suitable for bush, basket or standard, best in shade, among the most free-flowering doubles.

F. 'Baby Bright', Bright, UK 1993, corolla pale pink with pink veins, sepals pink, profuse single flowers, a neat, free-flowering small variety, popular for exhibition.

F. 'Constellation', Schnabel, USA 1957, almost pure white with slight tendency to turn to pink, medium to large double blooms, vigorous and free flowering with dark green foliage, a plant that makes a good bush, standard or pillar, best grown in cool shade for the finest white.

F. 'Countess of Aberdeen', Dobbie-Forbes, UK 1888, corolla, tube and sepals all white if grown in shade, otherwise a pink tinge develops, small pale green foliage, small single flowers in profusion on an upright plant, best grown as a bush or a standard.

F. 'Flowerdream', Rijff, Holland, 1983, ['Merry Mary' x 'Bora Bora'], corolla white, tube white with violet stripes, sepals white with pink undersides, profuse double flowers, bushy trailing plant with red stalks, for the best flower colour give it a bright position,

grow as a bush, standard or as a hanging basket subject.

F. 'Flying Cloud' (AGM), Reiter, USA 1949, corolla white slightly veined with pink at the base, tube and sepals white with slightly green tips, large double flowers with long 13mm (½in) tube, dark green foliage, a rather lax habit and so if growing as a bush it needs support, one of the first white double fuchsias from the USA, flowers best in sheltered shade and makes a good standard or bush, Barely hardy.

F. 'Frank Unsworth', Clark, UK 1982, corolla white slightly flushed with pink, tube and sepals white, small double flowers, small leaves, lax habit so best grown as a cascading subject in a tall container or hanging basket.

Fuchsia 'Mancunian'

ORIGIN: Goulding, UK 1985.
COROLLA COLOUR: White with pale pink flush and pink veins.
TUBE COLOUR: White ageing to red-pink.
SEPAL COLOUR: White tinged pink.
FLOWER FORM: Double.
FLOWER SIZE: Large.
HARDINESS: Tender to Barely hardy.

PLANT HABIT/GARDEN USES

This variety has a vigorous but lax habit so is best used as a single subject in large hanging baskets, or as a weeping standard, where its free flowering can be displayed to good effect.

NOTABLE FEATURES

The large flowers are a virtue although the white isn't as true as some others.

Fuchsia 'Cloverdale Pearl' (AGM)

ORIGIN: Gadsby, 1973 [Unnamed seedling x 'Grace Darling'].
COROLLA COLOUR: Pearl white with pink veins.
TUBE COLOUR: Pink-white.
SEPAL COLOUR: Pink shading to white with green tips.
FLOWER FORM: Single.
FLOWER SIZE: Medium.
HARDINESS: Tender to Barely hardy.

Fuchsia 'Cloverdale Pearl'

Fuchsia 'Margaret Tebbit'

NOTABLE FEATURES

Easy to grow and shape and a good and easy subject as a standard.

PLANT HABIT/GARDEN USES

An upright, self-branching variety with dark green leaves with red midribs.

Fuchsia 'Margaret Tebbit'

ORIGIN: Dyos, UK 1992.
COROLLA COLOUR: White.
TUBE COLOUR: Green-white.
SEPAL COLOUR: Pale pink.
FLOWER FORM: Double.
FLOWER SIZE: Medium.
HARDINESS: Tender to Barely hardy.

PLANT HABIT/GARDEN USES

The plant has a lax growth habit so looks good in hanging baskets but it can also be trained as a bush.

NOTABLE FEATURES

Attractive, pastel coloured blooms.

Other recommended varieties

The following are all Tender to Barely hardy unless otherwise stated.

F. 'Bountiful', Munkner, USA 1963, corolla white with pink veins, tube and sepals pale pink-white, double, medium-sized flowers, free-flowering, best grown in a hanging basket as it requires staking to support the heavy flowers if grown as a bush.
F. 'Evensong', Colville, UK 1967, corolla white, tube pink, sepals white with green tips, pale green leaves, single flowers in profusion, has a self-branching habit, best grown as a bush in a greenhouse or sheltered position.
F. 'Golden Anniversary', Stubbs, USA 1980, corolla deep blue-purple, fading to rich purple, splashed with pink, tube and sepals white, light green foliage, double very large flowers, long trailing stems make it ideal for a hanging basket.
F. 'Happy Wedding Day',

Fuchsia 'Neopolitan'

ORIGIN: Clark, UK 1984.
COROLLA COLOUR: White, pink, red.
TUBE COLOUR: White, pink, red.
SEPAL COLOUR: White, pink, red.
FLOWER FORM: Single.
FLOWER SIZE: Very small.
HARDINESS: Tender to Barely hardy.

PLANT HABIT/GARDEN USES

Needs pinching to make a decent upright shape; if left without attention, it develops a spreading habit. Best grown in small containers or train into a miniature standard.

NOTABLE FEATURES

The blooms appear in three different colours (red, pink and white) at the same time, indicating genetic instability. You may or may not appreciate the effect but there is nothing else quite like it.

Fuchsia 'Neopolitan'

Richardson, Australia 1985, corolla white, tube and sepals both white with pink markings, especially at base, double large flowers but not prolific, a lax habit but needs early pinching to develop a good shape, best grown in hanging basket or large pot.

F. 'Harry Gray', Dunnett, UK 1981 ['La Campanella' x 'Powder Puff'], corolla white with a little pink at the base, tube pink striped, sepals white with pink tinge at base and green tips, dark green foliage, double small-to-medium flowers, bushy habit that branches naturally, best grown in hanging baskets to show off the free flowering.

F. 'Hawkshead', Travis, UK 1962, corolla white, tube and sepals white with green tinge, deep green foliage, single very small flowers, upright bushy habit, Fairly hardy so can be grown as a garden shrub in many areas, the first pure white English-bred hybrid.

F. 'Igloo Maid', Holmes, UK 1972, corolla white with pink tinge at the base, tube white, sepals white with green tips, yellow-green foliage, double small-to-medium flowers that are self-cleaning, upright bushy growth, self-branching and free-flowering.

F. 'Linda Goulding', Goulding, UK 1981, corolla white with pale pink veins, tube white, sepals pink, red stamens provide colour contrast, single small-to-medium flowers, upright self-branching habit, prolific flowers that hold themselves horizontally rather than hang down, best grown as a bush or small standard.

F. 'Patience', Goulding, UK 1987, corolla white with slight pink tinge at base, tube and sepals white, double medium flowers of very fine form, mid-green foliage, upright, strong growing.

F. 'Pink Marshmallow', Stubbs, USA 1971, corolla white with pink veins and shading, tube and sepals pale pink, pale green leaves, very large double flowers, long trailing stems best grown in a hanging basket, possibly the largest flowered white variety.

F. 'Roy Walker', Walker, USA 1975, corolla white, tube and sepals white with pink flush, double medium flowers, late-flowering, compact short-jointed plant best grown as a bush in a container and kept in a warm greenhouse over winter.

F. 'Sleigh Bells', Schnabel, USA 1954, corolla white, tube white, sepals white with green tips, dark green foliage, single large flowers, free flowering with upright habit so makes a good standard, or grow it as a bush in the shade.

F. 'Snow White', Dunnett, UK 1982, corolla white, tube white with pale pink streaks, sepals white with green tips, double medium flowers, trailing habit so best grown in hanging basket or pinched hard to form a bush, best in shade.

F. 'Ting-a-ling', Schnabel-Paskesen, USA 1959, corolla white, tube and sepals white, single medium flowers, upright habit suitable as a bush or standard, the flowers tend to mark and discolour easily, prone to *Botrytis*.

Fuchsia 'Alf Thornley'

ORIGIN: Clark, UK 1981, ['Lilac Lustre' x a seedling].
COROLLA COLOUR: Cream-white.
TUBE COLOUR: Rose.
SEPAL COLOUR: Deep rose-pink.
FLOWER FORM: Double.
FLOWER SIZE: Medium.
HARDINESS: Tender to Barely hardy.

PLANT HABIT/GARDEN USES

Bushy upright growth, best grown in sun.

NOTABLE FEATURES

A very popular and widely used plant for exhibition.

Fuchsia 'Alf Thornley'

Other recommended varieties
The following are all Tender to Barely hardy unless otherwise stated.

F. 'Alice Hoffman', Klese, Germany 1911, corolla white with red veins, tube and sepals rose, dark bronze-green foliage, small single flowers, upright, vigorous and free flowering, Fairly hardy and in mild and sheltered areas can be grown in a border as a bush; in colder areas use it, as I do, for summer bedding or as a quarter standard.

F. 'Citation', Hodges, USA 1953, corolla white with pale pink veins at the base, tube and sepals pink, single large flowers of beautiful shape with petals that flare out, upright bushy habit, best grown as a bush, prolific flowers, can be tricky to grow well as it needs special attention to feeding and positioning without which the leaves tend to drop.

F. 'Collingwood', Neiderholzer, Germany 1945, corolla pure white, tube and sepals pale pink, double flowers, best grown as a container plant or as summer bedding.

F. 'Marilyn Olsen', Wilkinson, UK 1987, white or palest pink corolla, pink tube and sepals, single small flowers but freely borne, small upright habit.

F. 'Mayblossom', Pacey, UK 1984, corolla white flushed with pink, tube and sepals pink, double small flowers in abundance, bushy short-jointed habit, ideal for small hanging pots.

F. 'Mrs W. P. Wood' (AGM), Wood, UK 1949, corolla white, tube and sepals pale pink, light green foliage, single small flowers, upright free-flowering habit, hardy so can be grown as a low bush in the garden, best in light shade.

F. 'Nancy Lou', Stubbs, USA 1971, corolla pure white, tube pale pink, sepals pink with deeper pink undersides and green tips, double large flowers, upright bush with free-flowering habit, best grown in a greenhouse as a bush or standard when it can be spectacular.

F. 'Perky Pink', Erickson-Lewis, USA 1959, corolla white with pale pink tinge and pink veins, tube pale pink, sepals pink with green tips, double medium flowers, self-branching upright habit, free-flowering, easy to grow as a bush or as trained form.

F. 'Sophisticated Lady', Martin, USA 1964, corolla white, tube and sepals pale pink, double medium to large elongated flowers, free flowering on plentiful trailing stems so grow as a weeping standard or in a hanging basket.

F. 'The Aristocrat', Waltz, USA 1953, corolla white with pink veins, tube cream-white, sepals white with pink tips, double large flowers freely borne, upright bushy habit, best grown as a bush or standard.

F. 'Waveney Waltz', Burns, UK 1982, corolla white, tube and sepals very pale pink, light green foliage, single medium flowers, upright bushy growth ideal for growing as a bush or training as a standard.

F. 'White Spider', Haag, USA 1951, corolla white with slightly pink veins, tube pink-white, sepals pink with green tips, single flowers, best grown as a standard or in a hanging basket to show off the flowers.

Fuchsia 'Miss California'

ORIGIN: Hodges, USA 1950.
COROLLA COLOUR: White with pink veins.
TUBE COLOUR: Pink-red.
SEPAL COLOUR: Pink-red with darker underside.
FLOWER FORM: Semi-double.
FLOWER SIZE: Medium.
HARDINESS: Tender to Barely hardy.

PLANT HABIT/GARDEN USES

Upright growth that is suitable for growing as a bush or training as a standard. Shade from direct sunlight to prevent leaf scorch and fading of the flower colour.

NOTABLE FEATURES

One of the older white varieties still worth growing but best in light shade.

ABOVE: *Fuchsia* '**Miss California**'

BELOW: *Fuchsia* '**Tinker Bell**'

Fuchsia 'Tinker Bell'

ORIGIN: Hodges USA 1955 (but note that there is a more recent red and white British variety with the same name).
COROLLA COLOUR: White with slightly pink veins.
TUBE COLOUR: White tinged with pink.
SEPAL COLOUR: White with green tips, pink on undersides.
FLOWER FORM: Single.
FLOWER SIZE: Medium.
HARDINESS: Tender to Barely hardy.

PLANT HABIT/GARDEN USES

Lax habit but free flowering, may be grown as a bush or in a hanging basket.

NOTABLE FEATURES

Profuse and long flowering.

Fuchsia 'Brenda White'

ORIGIN: Pacey, UK 1986.
COROLLA COLOUR: White with pink veins.
TUBE COLOUR: Red.
SEPAL COLOUR: Red.
FLOWER FORM: Single.
FLOWER SIZE: Medium.
HARDINESS: Tender to Barely hardy.

PLANT HABIT/GARDEN USES

Best in containers or for bedding.

NOTABLE FEATURES

Very pretty, cup-shaped flowers, easy to grow, bushy and floriferous; there is also a form with variegated foliage but with white flowers, the effect is lost

RIGHT: *Fuchsia* 'China Doll'

Fuchsia 'China Doll'

ORIGIN: Walker and Jones, USA 1950.
COROLLA COLOUR: White with red blotches and veins.
TUBE COLOUR: Cerise with darker stripes.
SEPAL COLOUR: Cerise.
FLOWER FORM: Double.
FLOWER SIZE: Large.
HARDINESS: Tender to Barely hardy.

PLANT HABIT/GARDEN USES

Rather a lax habit so best grown as a trailing plant and good in a large basket.

NOTABLE FEATURES

Large and very distinctive flowers but not as profuse as in some more modern varieties even if you give careful attention to pinching.

RIGHT: *Fuchsia* 'Lady Thumb'

Fuchsia 'Lady Thumb' (AGM)

ORIGIN: G. Roe, UK 1967 [a sport of 'Tom Thumb'].
COROLLA COLOUR: White with carmine veins.
TUBE COLOUR: Carmine.
SEPAL COLOUR: Carmine-pink.
FLOWER FORM: Semi-double.
FLOWER SIZE: Small.
HARDINESS: Moderately hardy.

PLANT HABIT/GARDEN USES

An upright bushy habit on a low-growing plant; this together with its hardiness makes it a good rock garden subject provided you take care to choose its colour companions carefully. The plant is self branching and free flowering with neat dark green foliage and can also be grown as a bush or quarter standard.

Fuchsia **'Brookwood Belle'**

NOTABLE FEATURES

A sport of the well-known outdoor variety 'Tom Thumb' with similar flower shape and habit although the colour differs. Overall it is neither as hardy nor as robust as its parent.

Fuchsia **'Hula Girl'**

Other recommended varieties

The following are all Tender to Barely hardy unless otherwise stated.

F. 'Ballet Girl', Veitch, UK 1894, corolla white with some cerise veins, tube and sepals cerise, large double flowers in profusion, so plenty of impact although it needs pinching out to form a bush shape, upright vigorous habit, an old variety that has justifiably survived.

F. 'Bouffant', Tiret, USA 1949, corolla white with red veins, tube and sepals red, foliage has red veins, single flowers, easy to grow and propagate, its trailing habit makes it ideal for baskets or large containers, but for the best shape pinch regularly.

F. 'Brookwood Belle' (AGM), Gilbert, UK 1988, corolla white with red veins, tube and sepals red, medium double flowers in profusion, strong upright bushy habit so makes a large bush or standard.

F. 'Cardinal Farges', Rawlins, UK 1958, a sport from 'Abbé Farges' the only difference from that remarkably good variety being the flower colour, corolla white with light cerise veins, tube and sepals light red, medium single to semi-double flowers that are not only early and profuse but

have good rain resistance, Barely to Fairly hardy, upright, self-branching vigorous habit but the wood and leaves are brittle, can be grown in containers for exhibition or as a garden plant.

F. 'Hula Girl', Paskesen, USA 1972, corolla cream-white with pale pink veins and shading at the base, tube and sepals deep rose, foliage green with red undersides and red veins, large double flowers, a trailing free-flowering habit so best used in a large hanging basket or grown as a weeping standard.

F. 'Icecap', Gadsby, UK 1968, ['Snow-cap' x 'Bon Accorde'], corolla white with cerise veins, tube and sepals bright red, small to medium semi-double flowers, upright vigorous and bushy habit, makes a good standard and also a good exhibition variety.

F. 'Impudence', Schnabel, USA 1957, corolla white with carmine veins, tube and sepals carmine, single flowers with an unusual but elegant shape (the corolla's four circular petals open out wide and flat, the sepals are raised), upright habit but not self branching, needs early pinching to train into shape, best grown as a bush.

Fuchsia 'Madame Cornélissen' (AGM)

ORIGIN: Cornélissen, Belgium 1860.
COROLLA COLOUR: White with cerise veins.
TUBE COLOUR: Crimson.
SEPAL COLOUR: Crimson.
FLOWER FORM: Single to semi-double.
FLOWER SIZE: Small.
HARDINESS: Barely to Fairly hardy.

PLANT HABIT/GARDEN USES

An upright, bushy vigorous habit that is self branching and free flowering. It has dark green foliage with red veins. There is no need to shape the plant, simply grow it in groups of three outdoors to form a small bush shape.

NOTABLE FEATURES

One of the classic old European fuchsias and with a great deal of flowering impact for so hardy a plant.

Fuchsia **'Madame Cornélissen'**

Other recommended varieties
The following are all Tender to Barely hardy.

F. 'Molesworth', Lemoine, France 1903, corolla cream-white with cerise veins, tube and sepals bright cerise, double flowers, dark green foliage, very versatile and can be trained into any form including pyramids and pillars, notable for its neat flower shape and flowering impact.
F. 'Pacquesa' Clyne, UK 1975, (AGM), ['Pacific Queen' x 'Sheryl Ann'], corolla white with deep red veins, tube and sepals deep red, bright green glossy foliage, medium to large single flowers sometimes semi-double, upright, vigorous bush with fresh green foliage that responds well to pinching, noted for its flowering impact so makes an ideal bush specimen.
F. 'Pinto', Walker and Jones, USA 1956, corolla white splashed with deep pink, tube and sepals light red, very large double flowers, has a trailing habit so use it in a hanging basket or train as a weeping standard.

F. 'Rosecroft Beauty', Eden, UK 1969, corolla white with crimson veins, tube and sepals crimson, small semi-double flowers, pale green foliage edged with red and cream, small leaves, upright, bushy and free-flowering, not vigorous, best grown as a bush.
F. 'Spion Kop', Jones, UK 1973, named after the battle site in the Boer War rather than part of a well-known football ground, corolla white with rose veins, tube and sepals rose, medium double flowers, upright bushy habit that is self branching and free flowering, a good exhibition plant.
F. 'Strawberry Delight', Gadsby, UK 1970 ['Trase' x 'Golden Marinka'], corolla white with pink veins and petaloids white with pink flush, tube and sepals crimson, medium double flowers, yellow-green foliage with bronze sheen when young, an upright but lax habit so grow it as a bush or half basket. The foliage is inherited from 'Golden Marinka' and lends popularity to this variety although I find the combination too much.

Fuchsia 'Nellie Nuttall' (AGM)

ORIGIN: Roe, UK 1977.
COROLLA COLOUR: White with red veins.
TUBE COLOUR: Bright red.
SEPAL COLOUR: Bright red.
FLOWER FORM: Single.
FLOWER SIZE: Small.
HARDINESS: Tender.

PLANT HABIT/GARDEN USES

A vigorous variety with an upright habit reaching 15-45cm (6in-1½ft) in height. The flowers are upward-looking and are early and freely borne. Best grown as a bush.

NOTABLE FEATURES

Showy flowers on a very neat and compact plant.

Fuchsia 'Snowcap' (syn. F. 'Wendy') (AGM)

ORIGIN: Henderson, UK date of introduction uncertain but has been mentioned in written records from 1880.
COROLLA COLOUR: White with red veins.
TUBE COLOUR: Scarlet.
SEPAL COLOUR: Scarlet.
FLOWER FORM: Semi-double.
FLOWER SIZE: Medium.
HARDINESS: Barely hardy.

PLANT HABIT/GARDEN USES

An upright, vigorous habit with plenty of flowers and small dark green foliage. An easy variety to grow if you are prepared to pinch it early into shape. Can be grown as a bush, a very good standard or used as summer bedding.

NOTABLE FEATURES

An old variety whose strong growth and profusion of flowers has helped it retain its popularity.

Fuchsia 'Nellie Nuttall'

Fuchsia 'Snowcap'

45

Fuchsia 'Swingtime' (AGM)

ORIGIN: Tiret, USA 1950, ['Titanic' x 'Yuletide'].
COROLLA COLOUR: White with pink veins.
TUBE COLOUR: Scarlet.
SEPAL COLOUR: Scarlet.
FLOWER FORM: Double.
FLOWER SIZE: Large.
HARDINESS: Tender to Barely hardy.

PLANT HABIT/GARDEN USES

The growth habit is vigorous and upright initially but then under the weight of the flowers the stems droop and a more spreading habit emerges. It is a very versatile variety suitable for baskets or summer bedding, it can be trained as a bush, standard or espalier. The foliage is mid-green with red veins.

NOTABLE FEATURES

An extraordinarily popular variety to be seen everywhere in hanging baskets and a surprising plant in that its very full blooms are fairly weather resistant although the petals do turn brown eventually. It isn't until the flowers drop and must be swept up that you realise just how large they are. Undoubtedly one of the most outstanding varieties.

Fuchsia **'Swingtime'**

Other recommended varieties
The following are all Tender to Barely hardy unless otherwise stated.

F. 'Golden Swingtime', raiser unknown, UK 1981, [a sport of 'Swingtime'], identical to its parent apart from golden-variegated foliage which renders it hugely poplar, although I confess that I find the combination simply vulgar.
F. 'Texas Longhorn', Fuchsia-La Nurseries, USA 1960, corolla cream-white with cerise veins, tube and sepals scarlet, very large semi-double to double flowers, long buds up to 12cm (5in) open to sepals with a span of 15cm (6in) giving the appearance of windmill sails, foliage is large dark green with red veins, a trailing plant that produces few blooms, it is difficult to train so is usually grown in a hanging basket.
F. 'Tolling Bell', Turner, UK 1964, corolla white with cerise veins, tube and sepals scarlet, large single flowers, foliage has red veins, upright bushy vigorous habit and free flowering, best grown as a bush or a standard in a cool shady position.
F. 'Trase', Dawson, UK 1956, corolla white with carmine veins, tube and sepals carmine, medium double flowers, small foliage, upright, bushy, self branching and free flowering, best grown as a bush, Fairly hardy.

F. 'White Heidi Ann', a sport from 'Heidi Ann' that has occurred on several occasions with a white instead of lavender corolla, corolla white, tube and sepals deep pink, double flowers, makes a good bush or low garden shrub.
F. 'White Pixie', a sport of 'Pixie' that has been introduced many times (for example by Rawlins, UK 1967, Saunders, UK 1968, Merrist Wood College, UK 1968 and by Wagtails Nursery, UK as 'Wagtails White Pixie'), corolla white with red-pink veins, tube and sepals red, small single flowers, yellow-green foliage with red veins, upright, bushy free flowering, Barely hardy.

❝ There are almost as many variants of pink in fuchsia flowers as there are of red. I find it one of the more difficult colours to select: at one end of the spectrum, it can be harsh, assertive and verging on red, while at the other, little more than a faint blush to a white. In between come the colours that really are more appropriate to confectionery. Fortunately, most pink-petalled fuchsias have either white or pink tube and sepals; and there are a great many pink selfs (all-pink varieties). There are relatively few that combine pink petals with red, and very few indeed that combine pink petals with purple or orange. ❞

Fuchsia 'Hidcote Beauty'

ORIGIN: Webb, UK 1949.
COROLLA COLOUR: Pale salmon-pink.
TUBE COLOUR: Cream-white.
SEPAL COLOUR: Cream-white with green tips.
FLOWER FORM: Single.
FLOWER SIZE: Medium.
HARDINESS: Tender to Barely hardy.

PLANT HABIT/GARDEN USES

A strong-growing variety with an arching lax habit. Although it is reasonably free branching it responds well to pinching out. Large light green foliage. Grow it as a lax bush, in a hanging basket or train it as a standard or pillar.

NOTABLE FEATURES

Distinctive pastel flower colour.

Fuchsia 'President Margaret Slater'

ORIGIN: Taylor, UK 1972 ['Cascade' x 'Taffy'].
COROLLA COLOUR: Mauve-pink with a salmon pink flush.
TUBE COLOUR: White.
SEPAL COLOUR: White with rich pink flush and green tips.
FLOWER FORM: Single.
FLOWER SIZE: Medium.
HARDINESS: Tender to Barely hardy.

PLANT HABIT/GARDEN USES

This plant has a wonderful, naturally vigorous trailing habit that can be made

Fuchsia **'President Margaret Slater'**

Fuchsia **'Hidcote Beauty'**

use of in hanging baskets and standards. It flowers prolifically over a long period and the foliage is neat with red veins so overall it makes a very good garden plant.

NOTABLE FEATURES

It has inherited the profusion of flowers and trailing growth from its famous pre-war American parent 'Cascade'.

Other recommended varieties
The following are all Tender to Barely hardy.

F. 'Duchess of Albany', Rundle, UK 1891, corolla pale pink-cerise, tube cream-white, sepals cream-white with pink flush, light green foliage, medium single flowers, upright, bushy vigorous habit with plenty of flowers, attractive blooms but not for exhibition, best grown as a bush or a very fine standard.
F. 'Eleanor Leytham', Roe, UK 1974, ['Countess of Aberdeen' x 'Pink Darling'], corolla pink, darkening at the edge of the petals, tube and sepals pink-white, small glossy foliage, small single flowers, not easy to grow but a dainty plant as a bush or quarter standard.
F. 'Flirtation Waltz', Waltz, USA 1962, corolla pale pink, tube white, sepals white with pink undersides and green tips, light green foliage, double flowers, upright bushy vigorous habit, the plant is self branching and free flowering, ideal for training into a pillar or as summer bedding for a shady spot and also makes a fine standard, best in light shade as the flowers mark easily in sun.

Fuchsia 'Waveney Gem'

ORIGIN: Burns, UK 1985.
COROLLA COLOUR: Pink with a lavender flush.
TUBE COLOUR: White with pink flush.
SEPAL COLOUR: White with pink flush..
FLOWER FORM: Single.
FLOWER SIZE: Small to medium.
HARDINESS: Tender to Barely hardy.

PLANT HABIT/GARDEN USES

It has a neat rather bushy habit but it spreads out horizontally rather than growing upright so is best grown in a hanging basket or trained as a standard.

NOTABLE FEATURES

It offers a good contrast between its dark green foliage and flowers, thus making it a very popular show bench choice.

Fuchsia 'China Lantern'

ORIGIN: Raised 1953, believed American.
COROLLA COLOUR: Rose, white at the base, red-pink on the edges of the petals.
TUBE COLOUR: Red-pink.
SEPAL COLOUR: White with green tips.
FLOWER FORM: Single.
FLOWER SIZE: Medium.
HARDINESS: Barely hardy.

PLANT HABIT/GARDEN USES

Its habit is vigorous and upright then rather lax, the flowers are freely produced. Best grown as a container plant.

NOTABLE FEATURES

Whenever I have grown this variety, I have been struck by its dark green foliage as much as by its flowers.

ABOVE: *Fuchsia* **'China Lantern'**

LEFT: *Fuchsia* **'Waveney Gem'**

Other recommended varieties

The following are all Tender to Barely hardy unless otherwise stated.

F. 'Kernan Robson', Tiret, USA 1958, corolla salmon and pink, tube and sepals white with green, foliage dark green and glossy, large double flowers, the corolla is partly fused with the sepals, lush growth makes it is prone to grey mould (*Botrytis*), upright habit so grow it as a bush and support it with a few canes; well worth the effort for its exceptional flower colour and size.

F. 'Other Fellow', Hazard and Hazard, USA 1946, corolla pink with white at the base of the petals, tube white, sepals white with green tips, small single flowers, small foliage, upright bushy habit that is self branching, the flowers are small but profuse enough to be eye-catching when the plant is grown as a bush or for summer bedding.

F. 'Peachy', Stubbs, USA 1992, corolla pale orange-pink, tube and sepals white, very large double flowers.

F. 'Princessita', Neiderholzer, USA 1940, ['Fandango' x 'Mrs Rundle'], corolla very dark rose, tube white, sepals white with slight pink flush on the undersides, medium single flowers, a vigorous trailing habit with a profusion of flowers, ideal for containers or baskets.

F. 'Snowfire', Stubbs, USA 1978, ['Pink Marshmallow' x 'Fan Tan'], corolla bright pink to coral-pink with white markings, tube pink-white, sepals white with pink at the base and green tips, buds show rose-pink streaks before opening into large double flowers, large dark green foliage and red stalks, strong stems that tend to arch down, so a few early pinches will improve the habit, best grown in a hanging basket or as a bush (needs support) or as a standard, a striking flower colour combination.

F. 'Squadron Leader', Goulding, UK 1986, corolla white with pale pink flush, tube and sepals white, medium to large double flowers, lax growth but well branched making it ideal for a hanging basket.

F. 'Temptation', Peterson, USA 1959, corolla bright red-orange shading to white at the base of the petals, tube and sepals white with pink flush, dark green foliage, medium single flowers, stems are strong but the habit falls between an upright and a cascading type so tends to grow horizontally, the flowers are profuse but bloom in flushes unless the plant is given a large enough container, best grown as a bedding or container plant; although it is difficult to persuade a stem to train as a standard, once this has been achieved a good head of flowers is formed.

F. 'Whiteknights Pearl', J. O. Wright, UK 1980, [F. magellanica var. molinae x (F. magellanica var. molinae x F. fulgens)], corolla pale pink, tube white, sepals pale pink with green tips, foliage small and dark green, small to medium single flowers resemble F. magellanica but are larger, very vigorous upright growth and as it is Barely to Fairly hardy, it can make a good garden specimen. This is a very fine plant that has remained close in form to its parents.

Fuchsia 'Hampshire Leonora'

ORIGIN: Clark, UK 1991, [a double-flowered sport from 'Leonora']
COROLLA COLOUR: Pale pink with a deeper rose-pink at the base of each petal, darker veins.
TUBE COLOUR: Pink with darker veins.
SEPAL COLOUR: Deep rose-pink with green tips.
FLOWER FORM: Double.
FLOWER SIZE: Medium to large.
HARDINESS: Tender to Barely hardy.

PLANT HABIT/GARDEN USES

Stiff free-branching stems support a profusion of flowers. Makes a good bush or standard.

NOTABLE FEATURES

One of the best prize-winning standard fuchsias I have ever seen was of this variety.

Fuchsia 'Hampshire Leonora'

Fuchsia 'Andenken an Heinrich Henkel' (syn. *F*. 'Heinrich Henkel')

ORIGIN: Rehnelt, Germany 1897, [*F. corymbiflora* x 'Magnifica'], named after Heinrich Henkel of the German Henkel company that sold the plant.
COROLLA COLOUR: Deep rose pink.
TUBE COLOUR: Light rose pink.
SEPAL COLOUR: Slightly deeper rose pink-carmine-red.
FLOWER FORM: Triphylla.
FLOWER SIZE: Small.
HARDINESS: Tender to Barely hardy.

PLANT HABIT/GARDEN USES

A vigorous spreading bush. It is free-flowering with dark olive green leaves with dark red veins. Best when grown in a greenhouse.

NOTABLE FEATURES

Has inherited much of the merit of its magnificent species parent, *F. corymbiflora*, but tends to be rather more floriferous.

Fuchsia 'Display' (AGM)

ORIGIN: Smith, UK 1881.
COROLLA COLOUR: Deep cerise pink.
TUBE COLOUR: Pink.
SEPAL COLOUR: Deep rose pink.
FLOWER FORM: Single.
FLOWER SIZE: Medium.
HARDINESS: Barely hardy.

PLANT HABIT/GARDEN USES

A good bush variety with an upright vigorous growth that needs no support. It is very free flowering. Vigorous enough for all the larger forms of training including standards, pillars or pyramids.

NOTABLE FEATURES

Almost unicoloured flowers, a plant that does well as a summer bedder and overall one of the best of all fuchsia varieties; it should be in every collection; it has been in mine for many years.

Fuchsia 'Display'

Fuchsia 'Garden News' (AGM)

ORIGIN: Handley, UK 1978.
COROLLA COLOUR: Shades of magenta-rose, base of the petals are rose pink.
TUBE COLOUR: Pink.
SEPAL COLOUR: Pink.
FLOWER FORM: Double.
FLOWER SIZE: Large.
HARDINESS: Barely to Fairly hardy.

PLANT HABIT/GARDEN USES

A tall upright variety that is self branching. This free-flowering variety starts early and continues until the first frosts. Best grown as a container plant.

NOTABLE FEATURES

Surprisingly, one of the few double-flowered hardy varieties.

Fuchsia 'Garden News'

Other recommended varieties

The following are all Tender to Barely hardy unless otherwise stated.

F. 'Balkonkönigin', Neubronner, Germany 1896, corolla dark pink, tube pale pink, sepals pale pink with green tips, deeper pink undersides, small foliage with red veins, small single flowers, trailing habit that needs careful and frequent pinching out, free flowering.

F. 'Barbara', Tolley, UK 1973, a seedling from 'Display', corolla orange-pink, tube and sepals pale pink, medium single flowers but very prolific, self-branching so makes a good bush or standard, gives its best colour in the sun.

F. 'Beauty of Exeter', Letheren, France 1890, corolla rose-salmon, tube and sepals pale rose-salmon, yellow-green foliage, semi-double flowers, rather straggly habit but vigorous, will form a bush if staked, makes a good standard.

F. 'Beverley', Holmes, UK 1976, an unknown cross with 'Percy Holmes', corolla rich purple, tube rose, sepals rose with green tips, Barely hardy, medium single flowers, upright vigorous habit, good as a standard.

F. 'Billy Green' (AGM), raiser unknown but probably originated around 1966, corolla tube and sepals all salmon, triphylla flowers, lovely foliage colours in winter, upright and vigorous habit that needs careful pinching out early, makes a good standard.

F. 'Dusky Rose', Waltz, USA 1960, corolla rose-red ageing to rose pink, petals splashed with coral-pink, tube red-pink, sepals pink with green tips, large foliage, vigorous habit that is bushy and lax, self branching and free flowering, best grown in a hanging basket.

F.'Elfriede Ott', Nutzinger, Austria 1976, ['Koralle' x F. splendens], corolla, tube and sepals all salmon pink, foliage is dark green, triphylla type flowers, very vigorous upright habit, free flowering, not easy to grow but very showy.

F. 'Hobson's Choice', Hobson, UK 1976, corolla pale pink-white with darker veins, tube and sepals deep pink, large double flowers, very bushy upright habit that supports the flowers well, best grown as a bush or standard.

F. 'Iced Champagne', Jennings, UK 1968, corolla pale pink with darker veins, tube pale pink, sepals light pink with green tips, the foliage is large with red veins, medium single flowers, upright bushy vigorous habit that is self branching and free flowering, it has short internodes so is best grown as a container plant.

Fuchsia 'Hobsons Choice'

Fuchsia 'Jack Shahan' (AGM)

ORIGIN: Tiret, USA 1949.
COROLLA COLOUR: Rose pink.
TUBE COLOUR: Pale rose bengal.
SEPAL COLOUR: Rose bengal
with green tips.
FLOWER FORM: Single.
FLOWER SIZE: Medium.
HARDINESS: Tender to Barely
hardy.

NOTABLE FEATURES

Often confused with 'Jack Ackland' but
the latter is more upright and rigid with
a lighter pink flower.

Fuchsia 'Jack Shahan'

PLANT HABIT/GARDEN USES

With a natural trailing habit, this plant
is self branching and vigorous and is
one that I have had for many years. It
tends to flower on the ends of the
branches but flowering is profuse so it
makes a good basket plant and, with
care, a very good standard.

Fuchsia 'Pink Galore'

ORIGIN: Fuchsia-La Nurseries,
USA 1958.
COROLLA COLOUR: Pink .
TUBE COLOUR: Pink.
SEPAL COLOUR: Pink with green
tips.
FLOWER FORM: Double.
FLOWER SIZE: Medium.
HARDINESS: Tender to Barely
hardy.

PLANT HABIT/GARDEN USES

The foliage is dark green and glossy but
flushed with pink when young, while
the young stems are red. A natural
trailer, it needs regular pinching to
shape it so is best grown in a basket,
or trained as a weeping standard.

Other recommended varieties
The following are all Tender to Barely
hardy unless otherwise stated.

F. 'Leonora' (AGM), Tiret, USA 1960,
corolla pink, tube pink, sepals pink,
medium single flowers, upright bushy
habit, self branching and free flowering, suitable as bush or standard and a
good exhibition plant, best in cool
shade.
F. 'Liebriez', Kohene, Germany 1874,
corolla pink with deeper pink veins,
tube pale cerise pink, sepals cerise
pink, small single flowers, upright
bushy habit, self branching and very
free flowering, best grown in a small
container as a bush or trained as a
quarter standard, Fairly hardy.
F. 'Marcus Graham', Stubbs, USA

1985, corolla pink with pale orange
streaks although in the UK the colour
varies rather widely from pale pink in
the winter greenhouse to pale apri-
cot-orange in summer, tube white to
pink, sepals tinged pink, large double
flowers, long leaves up to 10cm (4in)
with pale green veins, upright sturdy
growth that makes a bushy plant or
standard, free flowering.
F. 'Orient Express', Goulding, UK
1985, corolla rose pink, tube pink-
white, sepals pink-white with red tips,
single triphylla flowers, upright habit
of moderate vigour, needs hard
pinching to create a good bush shape
but a popular show variety with its bicoloured flowers.
F. 'Perry Park', Handley, UK 1977,
corolla bright rose, paler at the base,

tube and sepals pale pink, medium
single flowers, upright bushy habit,
self branching with short internodes
but free flowering and can be grown
as a bush or makes good summer
bedding.
F. 'Pink Flamingo', Fuchsia Forest-
Castro, USA 1961, corolla pale pink
with deeper pink veins, tube pink,
sepals pink with green tips, dark
green foliage with red veins, new
growth is bronze, medium to large
semi-double flowers, rolled sepals on
long flowers are a distinguishing feature, free-flowering but with a lax
habit, the long stems need careful
pinching out and training, best grown
as a basket plant.
F. 'Pink Rain', de Graaf, Holland 1987,
corolla deep red-purple, tube and

Fuchsia **'Pink Galore'**

NOTABLE FEATURES

Beautiful flowers but neither freely borne nor vigorous and a tricky plant to over winter.

Fuchsia **'Traudchen Bonstedt'**

ORIGIN: Bonstedt, Germany 1905, [a *F. triphylla* hybrid].
COROLLA COLOUR: Pink, slightly darker than the tube and sepals.
TUBE COLOUR: Pale pink.
SEPAL COLOUR: Pale pink.
FLOWER FORM: Triphylla.
FLOWER SIZE: Long.
HARDINESS: Tender to Barely hardy.

PLANT HABIT/GARDEN USES

An upright, free-flowering habit ideally suitable for growing as a bush. The foliage is a light sage green with a red tinge beneath and on the veins, a feature that is always attractive.

NOTABLE FEATURES

Many dense clusters of flowers are produced continuously.

Fuchsia **'Traudchen Bonstedt'**

---

sepals rose pink, small single flowers, trailing habit, a very fine, very floriferous self-branching variety and ideally grown in hanging baskets.
F. 'Piper', Howarth, UK 1985, ['White Ensign' x 'White Spider'], corolla white, tube white with faint pink stripes, sepals white with pink tinge on undersides, foliage has red veins, medium double flowers, upright fairly vigorous habit, free flowering, best grown as a bush or trained as a standard.
F. 'Rebecca Williamson', Redfern, UK 1986, corolla pink striped deep peach and salmon, tube and sepals pink, large double flowers, best grown as a bush or in a basket.
F. 'Southgate', Walker and Jones, USA 1951, corolla soft pink with deeper

pink veins, tube pale pink, sepals pale pink, slightly deeper pink on the undersides and with green tips, large double flowers, upright (the stems are strong but arch), vigorous habit, free flowering, an easy-to-grow double pink with especially weather-resistant flowers, pinch out and grow as a bush or standard, one of the best double pinks.
F. 'Sugar Almond', Hobson, UK 1978, ['Angela Leslie' x 'Blush of Dawn'], corolla pale pink with rose pink flush, tube and sepals cream-white with pink flush, medium double flowers, upright vigorous habit, free flowering, makes a good bush shape if pinched early.
F. 'Susan Green', Caunt, UK 1981, corolla rose pink, tube and sepals

pale pink, medium single flowers, suitable for containers or as summer bedding.
F. 'Susan Travis', Travis, UK 1958, corolla rose pink, tube and sepals deep pink with green sepal tips, single flowers, a strong well-branched grower reaching 60-90cm (2-3ft), Barely hardy.
F. 'Waldfee', Travis, UK 1973, [a F. michoacanensis hybrid], corolla lilac-pink, tube and sepals lilac and pink, small 1cm (½in) long single flowers of Encliandra type, transparent tube allows the white and pink stamens and pistil to show through, silky sheen to foliage, a self-branching trailer or bush, vigorous and free flowering, Barely hardy to Fairly hardy.

Fuchsia 'Mieke Meursing'

ORIGIN: Hopwood, UK 1968, originally named 'Mrs Mieke Meursing' after a president of the Netherlands Fuchsia Society; a wonderful find, a chance seedling discovered growing near a plant of 'R.A.F.' which presumably features in its parentage.
COROLLA COLOUR: Rose pink with deeper veins.
TUBE COLOUR: Carmine red.
SEPAL COLOUR: Carmine red.
FLOWER FORM: Single to semi-double.
FLOWER SIZE: Medium.
HARDINESS: Tender to Barely hardy.

PLANT HABIT/GARDEN USES

The variety has an upright bushy habit that is vigorous and self branching. It is free flowering and may produce extra petals and sepals to give a semi-double form. The foliage can be marked by cold or draughts but this is no real drawback. Grow it as a bush or train it as a standard.

NOTABLE FEATURES

Exceptionally bushy and short jointed; should be in every collection.

Other recommended varieties

The following are all Tender to Barely hardy unless otherwise stated.

F. 'Beacon Rosa', Bürgi-Ott, Switzerland 1972, corolla rose pink with pale red veins, tube and sepals rose-red, dark green foliage, medium single flowers, upright self-branching habit, good rain resistance, best in a sheltered position, a sport from 'Beacon' (and may revert, something that is rather unusual in fuchsias) but with better colour although only Barely hardy.

F. 'Brighton Belle', Goulding, UK 1985, corolla salmon-pink, tube and sepals rose-red, medium single flowers of triphylla type borne in clusters, upright vigorous habit, self branching and free flowering, a good bush plant.
F. 'Nicola Jane', Dawson, UK 1959, corolla pale pink with darker veins, tube pink-cerise, sepals cerise with green tips, dark green foliage with red veins and red stems, medium double flowers, upright bushy growth, self branching and free flowering, easy to grow and ideal as a bush, Barely hardy.

Fuchsia **'Mieke Meursing'**

F. 'Prosperity' (AGM), Gadsby, UK 1970, ['Bishop's Bells' x 'Strawberry Delight'], corolla pale rose with rose-red veins and markings, tube and sepals shiny crimson, medium double flowers, dark green glossy foliage with red veins, upright vigorous habit that grows tall with few branches, free flowering, Fairly hardy, one of the few double hardy varieties (presumably the gene for doubling is linked with one for tenderness), so may be grown in the open garden or in containers as a bush or standard.

F. 'Rambling Rose', Tiret, USA 1959, corolla pink with deeper pink petaloids, tube pale pink with green flush, sepals pink with deeper pink undersides and green tips, medium-large double flowers, a natural trailer that is vigorous and very free flowering but needs pinching out and makes a good hanging basket plant.

F. 'Tausendschön', Nagel, Germany 1919, corolla light pink with red veins, tube and sepals red, foliage has red veins and red stalks, double flowers, strong growing, well branched and free flowering, ideal as a bedding fuchsia or in containers.

Fuchsia 'R.A.F.'

ORIGIN: Garson, USA 1942, surprisingly an American variety, from the same nursery as 'Winston Churchill' and named during the Second World War.
COROLLA COLOUR: Rose pink with cerise veins and markings.
TUBE COLOUR: Cherry red.
SEPAL COLOUR: Cherry red.
FLOWER FORM: Double.
FLOWER SIZE: Large.
HARDINESS: Tender to Barely hardy.

PLANT HABIT/GARDEN USES

The growth is upright then lax with red-veined foliage. This is a very free-flowering variety and will start blooming early and finish late but like several large-flowered forms, does need regular feeding to maintain its flower size. It can be grown in a pot, or hanging basket or trained as a standard.

Fuchsia **'R.A.F.'**

NOTABLE FEATURES

Profuse large flowers but I suspect that it is grown to some degree for sentimental rather than horticultural reasons.

Fuchsia 'Cambridge Louie'

ORIGIN: Napthen, UK 1978.
COROLLA COLOUR: Mauve rose pink.
TUBE COLOUR: Pale pink-orange.
SEPAL COLOUR: Pink-orange with green tips.
FLOWER FORM: Single.
FLOWER SIZE: Medium.
HARDINESS: Tender to Barely hardy.

PLANT HABIT/GARDEN USES

An upright, self-branching habit of moderate vigour. The plant is short jointed and very free flowering so can be grown for exhibition in a container or in the garden as a bush.

NOTABLE FEATURES

One of the most free-flowering varieties of this very unusual colour combination; a striking mixture of shades but one to place with great care.

Fuchsia **'Cambridge Louie'**

VARIETIES WITH MAINLY PURPLE PETALS

❝ This is a vast group because purple (embracing mauve, lilac, lavender and similar shades) is the characteristic fuchsia colour; there is after all, even a shade widely called 'fuchsia purple'. In truth, it isn't as widespread in wild Fuchsia species as red but in terms of chemical pigmentation, the two are very similar and so it has been relatively simple to produce purple-petalled plants even from red-petalled parents. Purple petals with white tubes and sepals make a particularly arresting, very modern-looking combination, purple petals with pink tube and sepals is becoming rather dated, all-purple flowers (purple selfs) are surprisingly rather uncommon, purple and red is fierce and fiery although with a noble touch, while purple and orange is a rare, acquired taste. ❞

Fuchsia 'Bealings'

ORIGIN: Goulding, UK 1983.
COROLLA COLOUR: Vivid violet.
TUBE COLOUR: White.
SEPAL COLOUR: White with pink undersides and green tips.
FLOWER FORM: Double.
FLOWER SIZE: Medium to large.
HARDINESS: Tender to Barely hardy.

PLANT HABIT/GARDEN USES

This is a very vigorous variety with an upright habit and is very free flowering. It is often used by exhibitors, responds well to pinching and can be grown as a bush or a standard.

NOTABLE FEATURES

There is an arresting impact from the strikingly contrasting flower colours.

Fuchsia 'Eva Boerg'

ORIGIN: Yorke, UK 1943.
COROLLA COLOUR: Pink-purple with pink markings, paler colour at the base of the petals.
TUBE COLOUR: Green-white.
SEPAL COLOUR: White with pink flush and green tips.
FLOWER FORM: Semi-double.
FLOWER SIZE: Medium.
HARDINESS: Barely hardy.

PLANT HABIT/GARDEN USES

An upright habit which then tends to be lax, self-branching and vigorous. There is a profusion of flowers yet the plant is easy to grow and makes a fine garden bush of around 60cm (2ft).

NOTABLE FEATURES

Still one of the most popular among the older varieties for its combination of hardiness and flower colour.

Fuchsia 'Bealings'

Fuchsia 'Eva Boerg'

Fuchsia 'La Campanella' (AGM)

ORIGIN: Blackwell, UK 1968, [a chance seedling at Blackwells Nursery of Swindon].
COROLLA COLOUR: Purple with cerise veins ageing to lavender.
TUBE COLOUR: White tinged with pink.
SEPAL COLOUR: White with pink flush on undersides.
FLOWER FORM: Semi-double.
FLOWER SIZE: Small to medium.
HARDINESS: Tender to Barely hardy.

PLANT HABIT/GARDEN USES

The plant has a lax bushy habit, it is short jointed and needs little training. It is, however, both very vigorous and free flowering and is best in hanging baskets or trained as a standard.

NOTABLE FEATURES

Versatile and easy to grow and propagate. Sets seed very readily and so has often been used as the seed parent in breeding.

Fuchsia 'La Campanella'

Other recommended varieties

The following are all Tender to Barely hardy.

F. 'Blowick', Porter, UK 1984, corolla purple, tube and sepals white with pink flush, single flowers, upright vigorous habit, free flowering, needs pinching to create a good shape.
F. 'Bon Accorde', (apparently known as 'Erecta Novelty' in the USA), Crousse, France 1861, corolla pale purple with white flush, tube and sepals white, single flowers, stiff upright small bush, one of the first varieties to hold its flowers erect, not self branching so early pinching is required, very free flowering and a valuable plant to use as an edging.
F. 'Bridesmaid', Tiret, USA 1952, corolla pale lilac-pink, darker towards the edge of the petals, tube white, sepals white with pink flush, medium to large double flowers, upright bushy growth, can be trained rather satisfactorily as a half standard.
F. 'Candlelight', Waltz, USA 1959, corolla violet and purple ageing to red, tube white, sepals white with slight pink flush on undersides, dark green foliage, medium to large double flowers, upright vigorous habit, self branching; thick foliage and succulent stems; prone to grey mould.
F. 'Capri', Schnabel Paskesen, USA 1960, corolla blue-violet, tube green-white, sepals white with green tips, dark green foliage with red veins, double flowers with very large petals, an arching habit that makes a good bush or trailer, needs protection to obtain the best from the big flowers.
F. 'Doreen Redfern', Redfern, UK 1983, corolla violet with white at the base of the petals, ageing to violet-purple, tube white, sepals white with green tips and pale lilac on undersides, small to medium single flowers, dark green foliage with pale undersides and white veins, an upright habit that is vigorous and free flowering, an ideal bush or small standard, best in cool shade.
F. 'Estelle Marie', Newton, USA 1973, derived from 'Bon Accorde', corolla pale violet-purple ageing darker, with white at the base of the petals, tube green-white, sepals white with green tips, small dark green foliage, small to medium single flowers held upright well out from foliage, upright bushy habit, self branching and free flowering, best grown as a bush.
F. 'Hermiena', Lavieren, Holland 1987, corolla deep purple, tube and sepals white, small to medium single flowers but profuse, trailing habit so best grown in a hanging basket.
F. 'King's Ransom', Schnabel, USA 1954, corolla deep purple, tube and sepals white, dark green foliage, medium double flowers, upright bushy habit, vigorous and free flowering, best grown as a bush or standard, one of the easiest of the purple-and-white varieties.
F. 'Louise Emershaw', Tiret, USA 1972, corolla red-purple ageing to cerise-red with tinges of pink at the base of the petals, tube white, sepals white with pale pink undersides and green tips, medium to large double flowers, large foliage, vigorous trailing habit and free flowering, best grown in a hanging basket or trained as a weeping standard.

Fuchsia 'Lady Patricia Mountbatten'

ORIGIN: D. Clark, UK 1985, ['Eden Lady' x 'Lady Kathleen Spence'].
COROLLA COLOUR: Pale lavender.
TUBE COLOUR: White to pale pink.
SEPAL COLOUR: White with pink flush, deeper on the undersides.
FLOWER FORM: Single.
FLOWER SIZE: Medium.
HARDINESS: Tender to Barely hardy.

PLANT HABIT/GARDEN USES

This variety has an upright habit with wiry stems and needs regular pinching to get a good bush shape. It is a more robust and disease-resistant variety than its parent 'Lady Kathleen Spence' (see page 60).

NOTABLE FEATURES

A pale but attractive flower; a good plant for a protected corner.

Fuchsia 'Preston Guild'

Fuchsia 'Preston Guild'

ORIGIN: Thornley, UK 1971.
COROLLA COLOUR: Violet-blue ageing to cerise, white at the base.
TUBE COLOUR: White.
SEPAL COLOUR: White.
FLOWER FORM: Single.
FLOWER SIZE: Small
HARDINESS: Barely hardy to Fairly hardy.

PLANT HABIT/GARDEN USES

A plant with an upright bushy habit. It is well branched, the foliage has red veins and it is very free flowering. Best grown as a bush or quarter standard, giving shade and shelter from rain damage.

NOTABLE FEATURES

Dainty bright flowers, the old and new blooms are very distinct.

Fuchsia 'Rose of Castile' (AGM)

ORIGIN: Banks, UK 1855.
COROLLA COLOUR: Red-purple shaded white at the base of the petals and with a white streak in the centre of each petal.
TUBE COLOUR: Waxy pink-white with green tinge.
SEPAL COLOUR: Waxy white with green tips, slight pink flush on the undersides.
FLOWER FORM: Single.
FLOWER SIZE: Small to medium.
HARDINESS: Barely hardy to Fairly hardy.

Fuchsia **'Rose of Castile'**

PLANT HABIT/GARDEN USES

The plant has a vigorous, upright bushy self-branching habit. It is free flowering with light green foliage and can be used for exhibition as a bush or standard.

NOTABLE FEATURES

An old variety with masses of flowers held horizontally, flowers from very early to very late in the season. There is another variety called 'Rose of Castille Improved' (Banks, UK 1869) (page 65) which is very different with corolla violet-purple, tube and sepals pink or light red, medium single flowers but less abundant than Rose of Castille', taller, stronger growth and hardier. But whether this constitutes an 'improvement' is a matter of taste.

Fuchsia **'Margaret Pilkington'**

Other recommended varieties
The following are all Tender to Barely hardy.

F. 'Malibu Mist', Stubbs, USA 1985, ['Ada Perry' x 'Trade Winds'], corolla blue-violet with light pink streaks ageing to purple with white at the centre of each petal, medium-large double flowers, tube white, sepals white with pink tinge on the undersides, foliage has red veins, a lax upright habit suitable for growing as a bush or in a basket.

F. 'Margaret Pilkington', Clark, UK 1985, corolla violet ageing to mauve, tube and sepals white with rose veins, single flowers, upright habit, vigorous and free flowering, a good exhibition variety.

F. 'Marin Glow' (AGM), Reedstrom, USA 1954, corolla dark violet with pink at the base of the petals, tube white, sepals white with green tips, dark green foliage, medium single flowers, upright bushy habit, vigorous, self branching and free flowering, regular pinching produces profuse flowers, so widely used for exhibition, outstanding colour but for best results grow in greenhouse or a sheltered position, as a bush or standard.

F. 'Minirose', De Graaff, Holland 1981, corolla light red-purple with light rose-red at the base of the petals, tube and sepals white with pink flush, small single flowers held out well, foliage has light red veins, vigorous upright habit, needs pinching out to obtain a good shape, a good free-flowering exhibition variety, best grown in a container or

trained as a small standard.
F. 'Pinch Me', (apparently sold as 'Phoenix' in Holland), Tiret, USA 1969, corolla purple shading to pink at the base of the petals, tube white, sepals white with green tips, light green foliage with red veins and stalks, medium to large double flowers, trailing habit but self branching and can be used in a basket or as summer bedding or trained as an espalier, free flowering but provide shade to obtain the best quality blooms.

F. 'Postiljon', Van Der Post, Holland 1975, [a seedling from 'La Campanella'], corolla rose-purple with white at the base of the petals, tube white with pink flush, and sepals white with pink flush and green tips, small single flowers that bloom early and carry on until the frosts, will flower through the winter in a greenhouse, a vigorous trailing habit that self branches and is free flowering, ideal for a hanging basket.

F. 'Ratatouille', De Graaf, Holland 1989, corolla purple with white stripe, tube and sepals pale lavender, large double flowers, best in a hanging basket.

F. 'Rose of Denmark', Banks, UK 1864, corolla rose-purple shaded pink at the base of the petals and with rose pink veins, tube white, sepals white with light pink flush and green tips, undersides are a deeper pink, medium single flowers in profusion, upright bushy habit but rather lax so needs pinching into shape for a bush or may be grown in a hanging basket or trained as a weeping standard.

Fuchsia 'Lady Kathleen Spence'

ORIGIN: Ryle, UK 1974, ['Bobby Shaftoe' x 'Schneewitchen'].
COROLLA COLOUR: Lavender-blue with light pink veins.
TUBE COLOUR: Cream-white.
SEPAL COLOUR: Cream-white with green tips, pale pink undersides.
FLOWER FORM: Single.
FLOWER SIZE: Medium.
HARDINESS: Tender to Barely hardy.

Fuchsia 'Lady Kathleen Spence'

PLANT HABIT/GARDEN USES

An upright bushy habit. Lush foliage that has the reputation of being especially prone to red spider mite. It has a lax upright habit that responds well to pinching but is hard to over winter as plants suffer die-back and cuttings are prone to grey mould (*Botrytis*). Place in shade for the best flower colour.

NOTABLE FEATURES

Delicately coloured flowers and a beautiful plant but not easy and it needs care to grow well.

Other recommended varieties

The following are all Tender to Barely hardy unless otherwise stated.

F. 'Alison Ewart', Roe, UK 1976, ['Eleanor Leytham' x 'Pink Darling'], corolla mauve with pink flush, tube pink, sepals pink with green tips, dark green foliage with red veins and bronze sheen, small single flowers, upright bushy habit, self branching, flowers early and in profusion, good for exhibition, best grown as a bush or quarter standard.

F. 'Blue Waves', Waltz, USA 1954, corolla blue-violet with rose pink markings and carmine veins, tube and sepals pink, light green foliage, large double flowers, vigorous upright habit, easy to grow.

F. 'Border Queen' (AGM), Ryle, UK 1974, ['Leonora' x 'Lena Dalton'], corolla deep purple-blue with pink flush fading to white at the base, darker pink veins, tube pale pink, sepals white with pink flush and green tips, red stems, small to medium single flowers, upright vigorous habit that is self branching and free flowering, best grown as a bush or standard, can be grown in a garden border in summer.

F. 'Brookwood Joy', Gilbert, UK 1983, ['Stanley Cash' x 'Joan Gilbert'], corolla clear blue with pink markings, tube white, sepals white with green tips, medium double flowers, a lax habit but if pinched regularly it can be shaped into a bush, prefers shade.

F. 'Carla Johnston', Pacey, UK 1986, corolla pale lavender, almost white, tube and sepals green-white flushed with light red, medium, single flowers that face outwards, stiff upright stems, free flowering, can be grown as a bush or a standard.

F. 'Caroline', Miller, UK 1967, 'Citation' is the female parent and contributes the distinctive flower shape, corolla pale lavender shading to pale pink at the base, tube pale pink, sepals pale pink with green tips and deeper pink undersides, large single flowers with flaring corolla, vigorous upright growth, makes a good bush if pinched out early, prone to grey mould (*Botrytis*).

F. 'Chillerton Beauty' (AGM), Bass, UK 1847, corolla purple ageing to magenta with pink veins, tube pale pink on the side that faces the sun yet cream on the shaded side, sepals pale pink with deeper pink undersides and green tips, small-to-medium single flowers, small leathery foliage, vigorous upright habit, self branching and free flowering, Fairly hardy and one of the classic old outdoor fuchsias, can be grown as large standard or bush. Remember that in 1847, when it was raised, greenhouses were only for the pleasure of the very wealthy.

F. 'Masquerade', Kennett, USA 1963, corolla dark purple with pink markings ageing to deep red-purple, tube green and white, sepals pale pink, deeper pink on undersides with green tips, medium double flowers, dark green foliage, a vigorous trailer, free flowering, best grown in a hanging basket, in a sheltered site or greenhouse.

Fuchsia 'Silver Breckland'

ORIGIN: Clark, UK 1995, [a sport from 'Breckland'].
COROLLA COLOUR: Silver-lavender.
TUBE COLOUR: White.
SEPAL COLOUR: Pink brightening towards the base.
FLOWER FORM: Single.
FLOWER SIZE: Medium.
HARDINESS: Tender to Barely hardy.

PLANT HABIT/GARDEN USES

An upright bushy plant with dark green foliage. Best trained as a bush.

NOTABLE FEATURES

Worth growing for its striking corolla colour but not a widely available variety.

Fuchsia 'Silver Breckland'

Fuchsia 'Cecile'

ORIGIN: Whitfield, USA 1981.
COROLLA COLOUR: Lavender-blue with pink at the base.
TUBE COLOUR: Pink.
SEPAL COLOUR: Pink-red with green tips.
FLOWER FORM: Double.
FLOWER SIZE: Medium.
HARDINESS: Tender to Barely hardy.

PLANT HABIT/GARDEN USES

A trailing habit ideal for a hanging basket.

NOTABLE FEATURES

A plant with a most appealing corolla colour that blends well with small blue-flowered bedding plants in baskets such as the trailing *Campanula isophylla*.

Fuchsia 'Cecile'

Fuchsia 'Deep Purple'

ORIGIN: Garrett, USA 1989.
COROLLA COLOUR: Deep purple.
TUBE COLOUR: White.
SEPAL COLOUR: White.
FLOWER FORM: Double.
FLOWER SIZE: Large.
HARDINESS: Tender to Barely hardy.

PLANT HABIT/GARDEN USES

A trailing habit so best grown in a hanging basket or train as a weeping standard. Very free flowering and becoming very popular.

NOTABLE FEATURES

A very valuable and easy variety; one that should be among the first for a beginner to try.

Fuchsia 'Deep Purple'

Fuchsia 'Lindisfarne'

ORIGIN: Ryle, UK 1972.
COROLLA COLOUR: Dark violet with deeper purple at the edge of the petals.
TUBE COLOUR: Very pale shell pink, almost white.
SEPAL COLOUR: Pale pink, almost white, with crimson at the base.
FLOWER FORM: Semi-double.
FLOWER SIZE: Small to medium.
HARDINESS: Tender to Barely hardy.

PLANT HABIT/GARDEN USES

A vigorous bushy upright habit. The plant is self branching and free flowering. It is used for exhibition and can be grown as a bush or standard.

NOTABLE FEATURES

This seems a particularly durable plant; I have had a specimen for longer than almost any other variety without deterioration.

Fuchsia 'Lindisfarne'

Other recommended varieties
The following are all Tender to Barely hardy unless otherwise stated.

F. 'Constance', Berkeley Horticultural Nursery, USA 1935, corolla rose-mauve with pink tints at the base of the petals, tube pale pink, sepals pale pink with green tips, small dark green foliage, medium double flowers of unusual round shape, bushy upright habit that can be trained into any shape except for baskets, free flowering, Barely hardy and one of the oldest of the outdoor American varieties still grown in Britain.

F. 'Danish Pastry', Fuchsia Forest, USA 1968, corolla salmon-red shading to lavender, tube coral-pink, sepals coral-pink with green tips, large single flowers, rather lax habit so needs staking and pinching to make a bush shape, better in a hanging basket.

F. 'Elsie Mitchell', Ryle, UK 1980, corolla light lavender with pink flush, tube pink, sepals pink but white towards the green tips, medium double flowers, lax upright self-branching habit, makes a good bush or small standard, also suitable for baskets, gentle colours that develop best in shade.

F. 'Lena' (AGM), Bunney, UK 1862, corolla purple, paler at the base, tube pale pink, sepals pale pink on top darker on underside with green tips, medium (though large for a hardy variety), single to semi-double flowers, a lax bush that is vigorous, self branching and free flowering, can be trained to most shapes but usually grown in a hanging basket, often develops flowers without petals in late autumn, Barely hardy to Fairly hardy, and also tolerant of dry conditions, a low spreading 30-60cm (1-2ft) high bush for the garden. The origins of this plant are matters of dispute but it is unarguably one of the classic hardy varieties. In a sheltered spot in my garden, one has survived through some of the harshest winters of recent years with little damage.

F. 'Melody', Reiter, USA 1942, corolla pale purple, tube and sepals pale rose pink, medium single flowers, upright bushy habit, very free flowering, train it as a bush or standard or can be used as summer bedding.

F. 'Micky Goult', Roe, UK 1981, ['Bobby Shaftoe' x 'Santa Barbara'], corolla mid-purple, tube white to pale pink, sepals pink darkening with age, light green foliage, small to medium single flowers, upright vigorous habit, self branching and free flowering over a long period, a well-proportioned plant used for exhibition and also for summer bedding.

F. 'Pink Darling', Machado, USA 1961, corolla pink-lilac lighter at the base of the petals, tube dark pink, sepals pale pink on top deeper pink on the undersides, small dark green foliage, small flowers carried rather horizontally, an upright vigorous habit but needs early pinching to form a good shape, very free flowering, best grown as a bush or quarter standard.

Fuchsia 'Paula Jane' (AGM)

ORIGIN: Tite, USA 1975.
COROLLA COLOUR: Red-purple ageing to deep red, with a pale pink flush near the sepals.
TUBE COLOUR: Very pale pink.
SEPAL COLOUR: Carmine-rose.
FLOWER FORM: Semi-double.
FLOWER SIZE: Small
HARDINESS: Tender to Barely Hardy.

PLANT HABIT/GARDEN USES

An upright bush that is vigorous and free-flowering. It makes a good exhibition plant and is usually grown as a bush although I've seen a find standard specimen too.

NOTABLE FEATURES

The purple of the corolla is more red than many and it ages rather attractively; too many fuchsias simply discolour a dirty brown with age.

Fuchsia 'Paula Jane'

Fuchsia 'Tennessee Waltz' (AGM)

ORIGIN: Walker and Jones, USA 1951.
COROLLA COLOUR: Lilac-lavender with pink petals.
TUBE COLOUR: Light red.
SEPAL COLOUR: Light red.
FLOWER FORM: Semi-double.
FLOWER SIZE: Medium to large.
HARDINESS: Barely hardy.

PLANT HABIT/GARDEN USES

The plant has an upright habit that is vigorous and self-branching. It is very free flowering and one of the easiest of fuchsias to grow. It shapes well so can be grown as a bush or standard.

NOTABLE FEATURES

The angular flowers have exquisite shape and are evenly distributed over the plant. A plant that must be on everyone's short-list.

Fuchsia 'Fuchsiade '88'

ORIGIN: De Graaff, Holland 1988.
COROLLA COLOUR: Rich red.
TUBE COLOUR: Dull red.
SEPAL COLOUR: Dull red.
FLOWER FORM: Single.
FLOWER SIZE: Small to medium.
HARDINESS: Tender to Barely hardy.

PLANT HABIT/GARDEN USES

The plant comes into flower early when grown as a garden shrub.

NOTABLE FEATURES

One of a number of Dutch varieties with intense red colours.

Fuchsia 'Tennessee Waltz'

Other recommended varieties

The following are all Tender to Barely hardy unless otherwise stated.

F. 'Margaret Roe', Gadsby, UK 1968, corolla pale violet-purple with pink veins, tube pale rose pink, sepals rose-red with green tips, small to medium single flowers held upright from the foliage, upright bushy habit, Barely to Fairly hardy, self branching, free flowering, grow it outdoors for the richest coloured flowers, can be grown as a bush, standard or as summer bedding.

F. 'Morning Light', Waltz, USA 1960, corolla lavender with pink markings ageing to rosy lavender, tube coral-pink, sepals coral-pink at base otherwise white with green tips, pale pink on undersides, large double flowers, yellow-green foliage with red veins, lax upright growth, a free-flowering, floppy habit best suited to hanging baskets or window boxes and best grown in a very sheltered site.

F. 'Rose of Castile Improved', Banks, UK 1869, corolla red-violet with deep pink veins ageing to red-purple, tube pale pink, sepals pink on top with green tips, deeper pink on the undersides, light green foliage, medium single flowers, upright vigorous habit, free flowering, best grown as a bush, standard or summer bedding. It is hardier in the open garden than 'Rose of Castile' (page 58) but otherwise not really an improvement.

F. 'Sparky', Webb, UK 1994, all-purple flowers, dark bronze foliage, single triphylla-type flowers held semi-erect, a slow-grower but makes an eye-catching feature plant.

F. 'String of Pearls', Pacey, UK 1976, [*F. lycioides* seedling], corolla pale rose-purple, tube pale pink, sepals pale pink with green tips, small single to semi-double flowers, upright vigorous habit, long arching stems that need pinching, free flowering but tends to flower at the tips, best grown as a bush.

F. 'Susan Ford', Clyne, UK 1974, ['La Campanella' x 'Winston Churchill'], corolla purple ageing to purple, tube and sepals deep rose-pink, dark green foliage, medium double flowers, the corolla stays closed, upright bush habit, self branching, free flowering, a good exhibition plant, best grown as a bush.

F. 'Taffeta Bow', Stubbs, USA 1974, corolla purple-violet, pink at the base, tube dark pink, sepals dark pink, large dark green foliage with red veins, large double flowers, a vigorous trailing habit, self branching, free flowering, best grown in a basket or trained as a weeping standard by stopping the side-shoots once.

F. 'Viva Ireland', Ireland, USA 1956, corolla lilac-blue, lighter at the base of the petals, tube and sepals pale pink, medium single flowers, bushy rather lax habit, self branching, free flowering, best grown as a bush, standard or as summer bedding.

Fuchsia 'Peppermint Stick'

ORIGIN: Walker and Jones, USA 1950.
COROLLA COLOUR: Purple with red and pink markings.
TUBE COLOUR: Light red.
SEPAL COLOUR: Light red, paler towards the tips.
FLOWER FORM: Double.
FLOWER SIZE: Medium to large.
HARDINESS: Tender to Barely hardy.

PLANT HABIT/GARDEN USES

The habit is that of an upright bush, it is self branching and very free flowering. A greenhouse variety that can be trained as a bush, pillar, pyramid or standard of any size. Also suitable for a hanging basket although it does not trail well.

NOTABLE FEATURES

A striking variety and one of the first fuchsias to be raised with tri-coloured flowers.

Fuchsia 'Peppermint Stick'

Fuchsia 'Abbé Farges'

ORIGIN: Lemoine, France 1901.
COROLLA COLOUR: Lilac-pink.
TUBE COLOUR: Light cerise.
SEPAL COLOUR: Light cerise.
FLOWER FORM: Semi-double.
FLOWER SIZE: Small.
HARDINESS: Barely to Fairly hardy.

PLANT HABIT/GARDEN USES

The growth habit is upright, vigorous and free-flowering but although the variety is self-branching, the branches are brittle and easily damaged. It is best grown as a bush or quarter standard.

NOTABLE FEATURES

Small but profuse flowers on upright growth; it may not sound much but I consider this one of the finest fuchsias ever raised.

Fuchsia 'Abbé Farges'

Fuchsia 'Army Nurse' (AGM)

ORIGIN: Hodges, USA 1947.
COROLLA COLOUR: Blue-violet with pink flush at the base and pink veins.
TUBE COLOUR: Carmine.
SEPAL COLOUR: Carmine.
FLOWER FORM: Semi-double.
FLOWER SIZE: Medium.
HARDINESS: Fairly hardy.

PLANT HABIT/GARDEN USES

A very vigorous plant that forms an upright bush with plenty of flowers. It is easy to grow in the garden or in a large pot.

NOTABLE FEATURES

Makes a large feature plant and is a very good outdoor variety.

Fuchsia **'Army Nurse'**

Fuchsia 'Dollar Princess' (AGM) (syn. 'Princess Dollar')

ORIGIN: Lemoine, France 1912.
COROLLA COLOUR: Purple, cerise at the base of the petals.
TUBE COLOUR: Cerise.
SEPAL COLOUR: Cerise.
FLOWER FORM: Double.
FLOWER SIZE: Small.
HARDINESS: Fairly hardy.

Fuchsia 'Dollar Princess'

PLANT HABIT/GARDEN USES

The growth habit is vigorous and produces an upright self-branching bush. This variety flowers early and profusely yet is easy to grow as a bush or garden plant.

NOTABLE FEATURES

Large mass of small well-shaped flowers; a very good variety from the same nursery as 'Abbé Farges'.

Other recommended varieties

The following are all Fairly hardy unless otherwise stated.

F. 'Achievement' (AGM), Melville, UK 1886, corolla red-purple, scarlet at the base of the petals, tube and sepals carmine-cerise, yellow-green foliage, medium to large single flowers, upright and vigorous habit, self branching and free flowering, responds well to pinching, Barely to Fairly hardy. An old variety, it has proved both durable and easy to grow.
F. 'Autumnale', Meteor, France 1880, corolla purple, tube and sepals scarlet, variegated foliage that starts yellow and green then ages to copper red, medium single flowers, stiff almost horizontal growth makes it difficult to train, Tender to Barely hardy.
F. 'Beacon', Bull, UK 1871, corolla bright mauve-pink, tube and sepals scarlet, large dark green foliage, medium single flowers that are borne early and continuously, upright bushy habit, self branching.
F. 'Bland's New Striped', Bland, UK 1872, corolla purple with red streak on each petal, tube and sepals cerise, dark green foliage, medium to large single flowers, upright bushy growth, self branching, best grown as a container plant, bush or standard, Tender to Barely hardy.
F. 'Brutus' (AGM), Lemoine, France 1897, corolla deep purple shading to carmine at the base, ageing to wine-purple, tube and sepals crimson-cerise, foliage has red veins, medium single flowers, vigorous upright bushy habit, free flowering, can be grown as a standard, pyramid or bush. Another example of the quite amazing skills of the Lemoine nursery.
F. 'Charming', Lye, UK 1895, ['Arabella Improved' x 'James Lye'], corolla purple ageing to red-purple, cerise at the base of the petals, tube carmine, sepals cherry red, yellow-green foliage, medium single flowers, upright vigorous habit, self branching.
F. 'Cliff's Hardy', Gadsby, UK 1971, corolla violet, lighter at the base with scarlet veins, tube crimson, sepals crimson with green tips, dark green foliage, medium single flowers that are held upright from the foliage, upright bushy habit, free flowering.
F. 'Cloth of Gold', Stafford, UK 1863, [a sport of 'Souvenir De Chiswick'], corolla purple, tube and sepals red, golden yellow foliage ageing to green with bronze flush and red undersides, small single flowers that are late into bloom and not prolific, upright bushy habit, Tender to Barely hardy.
F. 'Corallina' (AGM), Pince, UK 1843, [*F. cordifolia* x 'Globosa'], corolla purple but pink at the base of the petals, tube and sepals carmine, dark green foliage, medium single flowers, a vigorous spreading bush with lax habit, needs early staking.
F. 'Drame', Lemoine, France 1880, [a *F.* 'Riccartonii' hybrid], corolla purple-red, red at the base of the petals, tube and sepals scarlet, medium semi-double flowers, foliage yellow-green when young, vigorous upright bushy habit, self branching and free flowering, best grown as a bush.

Fuchsia 'Genii' (AGM)

ORIGIN: Reiter, USA 1951 [There is a view that this is a synonym of the variety 'Jeane'; it is also sometimes written 'Genie'. To confuse the issue further, there is also a quite distinct American variety called 'Genni'].

COROLLA COLOUR: Very dark purple ageing to red-purple.

TUBE COLOUR: Cerise.

SEPAL COLOUR: Cerise.

FLOWER FORM: Single.

FLOWER SIZE: Small.

HARDINESS: Fairly hardy to Moderately hardy.

PLANT HABIT/GARDEN USES

The growth is upright and vigorous with a self-branching and free-flowering habit. The yellow-green colour to the foliage is an acquired taste but certainly to obtain the finest colouration, it must be grown in full sun as it fades to green in shade. The plant is usually grown as a bush or as a garden shrub.

NOTABLE FEATURES

In my experience, this is one of the hardiest of all fuchsias and it is certainly one of the first to produce shoots in early spring. But you simply have to learn to like the colours.

Fuchsia 'Genii'

Other recommended varieties

The following are all Barely hardy unless otherwise stated.

F. 'Frau Hilde Rademacher', Rademacher, Germany 1925, corolla lilac-blue with cerise markings on the petals, tube and sepals scarlet, foliage has red veins, medium double flowers, upright rather lax habit, self branching and free flowering, can be grown as a bush if staked, or in a hanging basket.

F. 'Général Monk', raiser and date of introduction unknown, France, corolla blue-purple ageing to red-purple with pink veins and white shading at the base of the petals, tube and sepals cerise, small to medium double flowers, vigorous upright bushy habit, self branching and free flowering, easy to grow, usually used as an edging bush. Perhaps the chief claim to fame of this variety is its parentage of 'Heidi Ann' (opposite), one of the great modern fuchsias

F. 'Golden Treasure', Carter, UK 1860, corolla magenta-purple, tube and sepals scarlet, medium single flowers, variegated foliage of yellow and green with red veins, upright bushy habit, not many flowers and rather late into bloom, best grown as an upright bush or as summer bedding, Barely hardy to Fairly hardy.

F. 'Graf Witte', Lemoine, France 1899, [a hybrid of F. coccinea], corolla purple with cerise veins, tube and sepals carmine, small to medium single flowers, foliage yellow-green with red veins, upright bushy habit, free flowering, bush, Barely hardy to Fairly hardy.

F. 'Herald' (AGM), Sankey, UK 1887, corolla deep blue-purple with cerise veins ageing to red-purple, tube and sepals scarlet, medium single flowers, foliage has red veins, upright bushy, self branching and vigorous, easy to grow as a bush, garden bedding or as an exhibition plant, Barely hardy to Fairly hardy.

F. 'Howlett's Hardy', Howlett, UK 1952, corolla bright violet-purple with scarlet veins and paler at the base of the petals, tube and sepals scarlet, large single flowers, upright vigorous bush habit, free flowering, suitable for all types of training, or grown as a bush, Barely hardy to Fairly hardy.

F. Indian Maid', Waltz, USA 1962, corolla rich purple, tube and sepals scarlet, dark green foliage, medium to large double flowers, lax bush habit with long branches, free flowering, can be grown as a bush if pinched hard early or can be grown in a hanging basket, Tender to Barely hardy.

Fuchsia 'Gruss aus dem Bodethal'

ORIGIN: Teupel, Germany 1904.
COROLLA COLOUR: Dark purple, almost black on opening.
TUBE COLOUR: Crimson.
SEPAL COLOUR: Crimson.
FLOWER FORM: Single.
FLOWER SIZE: Small to medium.
HARDINESS: Tender to Barely hardy.

PLANT HABIT/GARDEN USES

The plant grows as an upright bush with a self-branching and free-flowering habit. It is easy to grow either as a bush or as summer bedding in a very sheltered position.

NOTABLE FEATURES

The flowers have an unusual colour combination and are individually particularly long lasting.

Fuchsia 'Gruss aus dem Bodethal'

RIGHT: *Fuchsia* 'Heidi Ann'

Fuchsia 'Heidi Ann' (AGM)

ORIGIN: Smith, UK 1969, ['Tennessee Waltz' x 'Général Monk'].
COROLLA COLOUR: Bright lilac-purple, paler at the base of the petals with cerise veins.
TUBE COLOUR: Crimson.
SEPAL COLOUR: Crimson-cerise.
FLOWER FORM: Double with numerous petaloids.
FLOWER SIZE: Small to medium.
HARDINESS: Fairly hardy.

PLANT HABIT/GARDEN USES

The growth is upright and bushy with a vigorous self-branching and free-flowering habit. The foliage comprises small leaves of dark green with red veins. Often grown as an exhibition plant, this variety makes a good bush or quarter standard. It can also be grown as a low-growing shrub at the front of a border.

NOTABLE FEATURES

A profuse early flowering variety that has a dense bushy habit.

Fuchsia 'Lady Isobel Barnett'

ORIGIN: Gadsby, UK 1968.
COROLLA COLOUR: Rose-purple with purple edges to the petals.
TUBE COLOUR: Rose-red.
SEPAL COLOUR: Rose-red.
FLOWER FORM: Single.
FLOWER SIZE: Medium.
HARDINESS: Tender to Barely hardy.

PLANT HABIT/GARDEN USES

A very vigorous plant with an upright bushy habit. The plant is well branched and the enormously prolific blooms are held well out from the foliage.

NOTABLE FEATURES

The strong growth and masses of well presented flowers make this an ideal variety for pyramid training. It has been described as the most floriferous of all fuchsias.

Fuchsia 'Lady Isobel Barnett'

Fuchsia 'Mrs Popple' (AGM)

ORIGIN: Elliott, UK 1899.
COROLLA COLOUR: Violet-purple, paler at the base of the petals and with light cerise veins.
TUBE COLOUR: Scarlet.
SEPAL COLOUR: Scarlet.
FLOWER FORM: Single.
FLOWER SIZE: Medium.
HARDINESS: Fairly hardy to Moderately hardy.

PLANT HABIT/GARDEN USES

The plant has an upright bushy habit and it is vigorous and free flowering. The dark green leaves are small and narrow. It can be grown as a bush, a standard or as a garden shrub where it is one of the first to flower and makes a good hedge up to about 1.2m (4ft).

NOTABLE FEATURES

One of the hardiest fuchsias and one of the most famous of all varieties. Almost certainly, the most widely grown hardy variety in Britain.

Fuchsia 'Mrs Popple'

Other recommended varieties
The following are all Tender to Barely hardy unless otherwise stated.

F. 'Lady Boothby', Raffill, UK 1939, [*F. alpestris* x 'Royal Purple'], corolla very dark purple, almost black on opening but pink at the base of the petals with cerise veins, tube and sepals crimson, small single flowers, dark green foliage, very vigorous upright habit, long branches with long internodes so needs regular pinching, best grown as a climber against a support, free flowering, Fairly to Moderately hardy.
F. 'Loeky', De Graaff, Holland 1979, ['Joy Patmore' x 'Impudence'], corolla blue ageing to lilac-blue, slightly paler at the base of the petals and with light veins, tube white with faint pink tinge, sepals white with tinge of rose pink with deeper pink on the undersides and green tips, medium double flowers of an unusual shape like a plate, natural trailing habit with thin stems, free flowering, best grown in a hanging basket in a shaded position.
F. 'Margaret Brown' (AGM), Wood, UK 1949, corolla pale rose pink with deeper veins, tube and sepals rose pink, small single flowers, upright bushy habit, self branching and free flowering, best grown as a bush or summer bedding plant, Fairly hardy.

Fuchsia 'Riccartonii' (AGM)
(syn. *F. magellanica* 'Riccartonii')

Fuchsia **'Riccartonii'**

ORIGIN: Young, UK 1830, [a hybrid developed in Riccarton near Edinburgh from 'Globosa' x *F. macrostema*].
COROLLA COLOUR: Deep purple.
TUBE COLOUR: Bright red.
SEPAL COLOUR: Bright red.
FLOWER FORM: Single.
FLOWER SIZE: Medium.
HARDINESS: Fairly hardy to Moderately hardy.

PLANT HABIT/GARDEN USES

Often grown as a hedge and certainly best outside as the leaves drop when it is grown in a greenhouse.

NOTABLE FEATURES

A hardy, strong-growing variety that can reach 1.5-2m (5-6½ft). The foliage has a particularly attractive bronze sheen.

F. 'Margaret' (AGM), Wood, UK 1937, [*F. magellanica* var. *molinae* x 'Heritage'], corolla violet-purple with cerise veins, pink at the base of the petals, tube and sepals carmine-red, medium double flowers, very vigorous upright growth, self branching and free flowering, best grown as a bush or a garden shrub, Fairly hardy and in mild areas will form a fine plant up to 6m (20ft) high.

F. 'Mission Bells', Walker and Jones, USA 1948, corolla vivid purple with cerise markings at the base of the petals, tube and sepals scarlet, dark green foliage, medium to large single flowers, vigorous upright bush, self branching and free flowering, best grown as a bush or as summer bedding, can be trained as a standard but older wood is brittle, Barely hardy.

F. 'Mr A. Huggett', raiser and date of introduction not known, corolla pink-purple, deeper at the edges of the petals and pink at the base, tube and sepals red, small-to-medium single flowers, large foliage, vigorous upright bush, self branching and free flowering, good exhibition variety or grow as a bush, Barely to Fairly hardy.

F. 'Papoose', Reedstrom, USA 1960, corolla very dark purple, lighter at the base of the petals, tube and sepals scarlet, small single flowers, small narrow foliage, rather lax bushy habit but it is easy to train, free flowering and can be grown as a bush or quarter standard, Fairly hardy.

F. 'Pink Fantasia', Webb, UK 1989, corolla purple, tube and sepals pink, medium single flowers, vigorous upright bushy habit, but needs pinching to produce a plant for exhibition.

F. 'Pixie', Russell, UK 1960, [a sport of 'Graf Witte'], corolla mauve-purple with carmine veins, slightly paler shading at the base of the petals, tube carmine-red, sepals carmine, small-to-medium single flowers, foliage yellow-green with red veins, upright bushy habit, self branching and free flowering, can be grown as a bush or a garden shrub, Barely to Fairly hardy, also good for exhibition.

Fuchsia 'Royal Velvet' (AGM)

ORIGIN: Waltz, USA 1962.
COROLLA COLOUR: Deep purple with outer petals with crimson markings.
TUBE COLOUR: Crimson.
SEPAL COLOUR: Crimson.
FLOWER FORM: Double.
FLOWER SIZE: Medium to large.
HARDINESS: Tender to Barely hardy

PLANT HABIT/GARDEN USES

This is a vigorous plant with an upright bushy habit that is self branching and free flowering. It can be grown as a strong bush if pinched out regularly but also makes a good standard and exhibition plant.

NOTABLE FEATURES

The corolla opens widely and attractively to reveal a red centre.

Fuchsia 'Royal Velvet'

Other recommended varieties

The following are all Tender to Barely hardy unless otherwise stated.

F. 'Royal Purple', Lemoine, France 1896, corolla purple, slightly paler at the base of the petals with red veins, tube and sepals cerise, medium-to-large single to semi-double flowers, upright bushy habit, vigorous, free flowering, a versatile plant that can be grown in a tub, trained into a standard or pyramid or even allowed to climb, Fairly hardy.

F. 'Ruth King', Tiret, USA 1967, corolla lilac and white, tube pink, sepals pink, large double flowers, a vigorous trailing habit, free flowering, best grown in a hanging basket.

F. 'Scarcity', Lye, UK 1869, corolla deep purple, shaded scarlet at the base of the petals, tube and sepals deep scarlet, medium single flowers, upright bushy habit, self branching and free flowering, can be grown as a bush, Fairly hardy.

F. 'Sealand Prince', Bees, UK 1967, corolla pale violet-purple ageing to red-purple, tube and sepals light red, small-to-medium single flowers, vigorous upright bushy habit, free flowering, best grown in the open ground rather than in a container, Barely hardy.

F. 'Son of Thumb' (AGM), Gubler, UK 1978, [a sport of 'Tom Thumb'], corolla lilac, tube and sepals cerise, small single/semi-double flowers, good exhibition plant in small pots, Fairly hardy and identical to 'Tom Thumb' in all except size but has never achieved the popularity and status of its better known

and very much older parent.

F. 'Swanley Gem' (AGM), Cannell, UK 1901, corolla violet with red veins, paler shade of scarlet at the base of the petals, tube and sepals scarlet, medium single flowers that are saucer shaped, small-leaved foliage, upright bushy habit, self branching and free flowering, a good exhibition variety or may be grown as a bush.

F. 'Tom West', Meillez, France 1853, corolla purple, tube and sepals red, small single flowers that appear late in the season, foliage variegated pale grey-green and cream, upright lax habit, best grown in hanging baskets for its foliage, Fairly hardy.

F. 'Trail Blazer', Reiter, USA 1951, corolla rose-mauve, paler at the base of the petals, tube and sepals crimson, medium-to-large double flowers, a vigorous trailing habit, self branching and free flowering, best grown in a hanging basket or trained as a weeping standard.

F. 'Tropic Sunset', Antonelli, USA 1965, corolla dark purple, pale at the base of the petals with pink markings, tube and sepals carmine, small-to-medium double flowers, red-bronze foliage tipped with green, red stems, vigorous trailing habit, self branching and free flowering.

F. 'Voodoo', Tiret, USA 1953, corolla dark purple-violet, tube and sepals dark red, large double flowers, vigorous upright habit, self branching and free flowering, best grown as a bush but requires support and I find that the small twiggy branches pushed in among the the emerging fruits provide this most satisfactorily.

Fuchsia 'Tom Thumb' (AGM)

ORIGIN: Baudinat, France 1850.
COROLLA COLOUR: Mauve-purple.
TUBE COLOUR: Carmine.
SEPAL COLOUR: Carmine.
FLOWER FORM: Single to semi-double.
FLOWER SIZE: Small.
HARDINESS: Fairly hardy.

PLANT HABIT/GARDEN USES

This variety has an upright bushy growth that is self branching and free flowering. It is very versatile being both a good exhibition plant as a bush or quarter standard and a garden plant.

NOTABLE FEATURES

One of the most famous of the old hardy fuchsias and perhaps the best of all for smaller gardens as it is a dwarf variety that reaches no more than about 45cm (1½ft).

Fuchsia **'Tom Thumb'**

Fuchsia 'Daisy Bell'

ORIGIN: Raiser unknown introduced by Miescke, USA 1977.
COROLLA COLOUR: Vermilion shading to orange at the base of the petals
TUBE COLOUR: White with an orange tinge.
SEPAL COLOUR: Pale orange with green tips.
FLOWER FORM: Single.
FLOWER SIZE: Small.
HARDINESS: Tender to Barely hardy.

PLANT HABIT/GARDEN USES

The foliage is rather an acquired taste, being variegated light green and copper with red veins. This is a natural trailer that is self branching and free flowering so it is ideal for a hanging basket, but for the best flower colour, position the plant in a sunny site.

NOTABLE FEATURES

A pretty and unusual variety, ideal for baskets.

Fuchsia **'Daisy Bell'**

VARIETIES WITH MAINLY RED PETALS

Although purple is the commonest colour for fuchsias in cultivation, red is commoner in the wild species but the fuchsia reds, like most shades of botanical red, are never easy to blend with other flower colours. As fuchsias are so frequently grown in close proximity to other flowers, especially in containers, this is a very real challenge. The truly startling varieties are those like 'Frosted Flame' with red petals and white tube and these need to be placed with especial care. Red and pink can be an attractive combination provided the two are from similar parts of the spectrum; a red close to orange with a pink close to purple can create a very different impact.

Fuchsia 'Bow Bells'

ORIGIN: Handley, UK 1972.
COROLLA COLOUR: Magenta with white at the base of the petals.
TUBE COLOUR: White.
SEPAL COLOUR: White with green tips.
FLOWER FORM: Single to semi-double.
FLOWER SIZE: Large.
HARDINESS: Tender to Barely hardy.

Fuchsia 'Bow Bells'

PLANT HABIT/GARDEN USES

The upright self-branching growth makes a good spreading bush.

NOTABLE FEATURES

The large flowers are produced early and in large numbers.

Fuchsia 'Seventh Heaven'

Fuchsia 'Seventh Heaven'

ORIGIN: Stubbs, USA 1981, ['Pepi' x 'Applause'].
COROLLA COLOUR: Red with white markings at the base.
TUBE COLOUR: White.
SEPAL COLOUR: White with pink tinge.
FLOWER FORM: Double.
FLOWER SIZE: Large.
HARDINESS: Tender to Barely hardy.

PLANT HABIT/GARDEN USES

A vigorous plant with strong stiff growth that arches down as it grows. It is best grown in a large tub or hanging basket but could be trained as a standard.

NOTABLE FEATURES

Large flowers of a very intense colour but not especially free flowering.

Fuchsia 'Lillibet'

ORIGIN: Hodges, USA 1954.
COROLLA COLOUR: Rose pink.
TUBE COLOUR: White with a pink flush.
SEPAL COLOUR: White with a pink flush on the undersides.
FLOWER FORM: Double.
FLOWER SIZE: Large.
HARDINESS: Tender to Barely hardy.

PLANT HABIT/GARDEN USES

This plant has a vigorous trailing habit with long internodes, so for the best effect, rather than training it, allow to it grow naturally in a fairly large hanging basket. It is free flowering, the blooms are heavy and hang down even when in bud.

NOTABLE FEATURES

One of the best pink-and-white flowered fuchsias although many people find its growth habit ungainly and it can be prone to rain damage.

Fuchsia 'Lillibet'

Other recommended varieties
The following are all Tender to Barely hardy.

F. 'Cascade', Lagen, USA 1937 ['Rolla' x 'Amy Lye'], corolla dark carmine-red, tube and sepals white with carmine flush, light green foliage, large single flowers that are long and pendulous, cascading self-branching habit with flowers in profusion, a good sub-ject for a hanging basket or weeping standard and a variety that I have grown for as long as I have grown fuchsias.

F. 'Florentina', Tiret, USA 1960, corolla deep red with white at the base of the petals, tube green-white, sepals white with green tips, the foliage has red veins and stalks, large double flowers, a natural trailer, free flowering, best in a hanging basket.

F. 'Frosted Flame', Handley, UK 1975, corolla bright flame red with deeper edge but pale pink nearer the tube, tube white, sepals white with pale pink flush on undersides, large single flowers, a natural trailer, self branching and free flowering, flowers early, best grown in shade for the finest flower colour, ideal in hanging baskets where you want to create something with real impact.

Fuchsia 'Checkerboard' (AGM)

ORIGIN: Walker and Jones, USA 1948.
COROLLA COLOUR: Red with white at the base.
TUBE COLOUR: Deep red.
SEPAL COLOUR: White with red at the base.
FLOWER FORM: Single.
FLOWER SIZE: Medium.
HARDINESS: Tender to Barely hardy.

PLANT HABIT/GARDEN USES

A very vigorous plant with long internodes, making it unsuitable for close pinching. Its upright habit renders it ideal for training as a standard or as summer bedding. The flowers are produced in profusion.

NOTABLE FEATURES

As its name suggests, the contrast between the red and white is very striking.

Other recommended varieties
The following are all Tender to Barely hardy.

F. 'Cheers', Stubbs, USA 1979, corolla orange and red, tube and sepals coral-pink, foliage dark green, medium double flowers, vigorous lax to upright bush habit that needs tying down to persuade it to trail, best in a sheltered position.
F. 'Coachman', Bright, UK date unknown, corolla orange-vermilion, tube salmon pink, sepals salmon pink with green tips, foliage light green, large leaves, medium single flowers, self branching, medium upright habit that can be trained, early flowers in profusion but blooms in marked flushes, best in a sunny position.
F. 'Come Dancing', Handley, UK 1972, corolla magenta-rose with salmon-rose at the base, tube and sepals deep pink, foliage bright green and crinkled, large double flowers, vigorous spreading bush, self branching, can be grown as a bush or tied down to use in a basket, flowers over a long period.
F. 'Coquet Dale', Ryle, UK 1976, ['Joe Kusber' x 'Northumbrian Belle'], corolla lilac, tube pink-white, sepals rose, medium double flowers, vigorous upright bush, self branching, best grown as bush or standard.
F. 'Flying Scotsman', Goulding, UK 1985, corolla red with white markings, tube white with pale pink flush, sepals dark pink on top, lighter on the undersides, medium-to-large double flowers, vigorous upright habit, free flowering, makes a good

Fuchsia 'Checkerboard'

bush if pinched out, can also be trained as a standard.

F. 'Gay Parasol', Stubbs, USA 1979, dark red-purple ageing to bright red-purple, tube ivory-green, sepals ivory with faint magenta streaks down the edges ageing to ivory with magenta flush, red veins to foliage, medium double flowers, light-coloured buds make a strong contrast with dark open blooms, self-branching upright habit, makes a good bush.

F. 'Joy Patmore' (AGM), Turner, UK 1961, corolla cerise with white at the base of the petals and darker at the edges, tube white, sepals white with green tips, dark green foliage, medium single flowers, upright small bushy habit, self branching and free flowering, a good exhibition variety,

as bush or standard, best grown in greenhouse.

F. 'La Fiesta', Kennett, USA 1962, corolla red-purple with white petaloids with cerise markings, tube white, sepals white with green tips, foliage dark green, medium-to-large double flowers, a vigorous trailer, self branching and free flowering, ideal for hanging baskets but choose a sheltered position.

F. 'Rosy Frills', Handley, UK 1979, corolla deep rose edged red on the outer petals with salmon markings, tube green-white, sepals very pale pink with pale yellow-green tips, foliage is dark green with red stems and veins, large double flowers, lax bush with a spreading habit, early flowers in profusion, ideal for basket.

Fuchsia 'Joy Patmore'

Fuchsia 'Jennie Rachael'

ORIGIN: Cheetham, UK 1979.
COROLLA COLOUR: Rose red.
TUBE COLOUR: White.
SEPAL COLOUR: White with slight pink tinge.
FLOWER FORM: Double.
FLOWER SIZE: Large.
HARDINESS: Tender to Barely hardy.

PLANT HABIT/GARDEN USES

The plant has strong upright stems. The leaves are particularly large and reach 12cm (5in) in length.

NOTABLE FEATURES

The foliage is perhaps the most impressive feature of this variety.

Fuchsia 'Auntie Jinks'

ORIGIN: Wilson, UK 1970, [a seedling from 'Checkerboard'].
COROLLA COLOUR: Purple with white shading.
TUBE COLOUR: Pink-red.
SEPAL COLOUR: White edged with cerise.
FLOWER FORM: Single.
FLOWER SIZE: Small.
HARDINESS: Tender to Barely hardy.

PLANT HABIT/GARDEN

USES: This plant has a pendulous habit so is best suited to a hanging basket. Although the flowers are small they are borne in profusion and act as a foil for the small dark green foliage.

Fuchsia 'Auntie Jinks'

NOTABLE FEATURES

I find this one of the most reliable of all smaller-flowered hanging basket varieties.

Fuchsia 'Sunray'

ORIGIN: Milner, UK 1872.
COROLLA COLOUR: Purple-
cerise.
TUBE COLOUR: Red.
SEPAL COLOUR: Dark pink
on top, a darker shade on the
undersides.
FLOWER FORM: Single.
FLOWER SIZE: Small.
HARDINESS: Tender to Barely
hardy.

PLANT HABIT/GARDEN USES

The plant has an upright bushy habit
and moderate vigour. The foliage is
light green with cream-white edges and
a red flush but the foliage varies
depending on the growing conditions.
The flowers are insignificant. It is easy
to grow either in a greenhouse or in
the garden and can be shaped if

Fuchsia **'Sunray'**

required, but needs frost-free conditions over winter.

NOTABLE FEATURES

Grown mainly for its colourful foliage.

Fuchsia 'Bergnimf'

ORIGIN: Appel, Holland 1981,
[*F. sessilifolia* x *F. fulgens*].
COROLLA COLOUR: Red.
TUBE COLOUR: Rose-red.
SEPAL COLOUR: Bright rose-red.
FLOWER FORM: Single.
FLOWER SIZE: Small.
HARDINESS: Tender to Barely
hardy.

PLANT HABIT/GARDEN USES

A strong-growing plant but with a
markedly upright habit and not easy to
train into a shape. The foliage is dark
green and similar to that of its parent,
F. sessilifolia, but larger.

NOTABLE FEATURES

Like many of the red-flowered fuchsias,
the contrast between the flowers and
the foliage is the most striking feature.

Other recommended varieties
The following are all Tender to Barely
hardy unless otherwise stated.

F. 'Brilliant', Bull, UK 1865, corolla
violet-magenta with red veins, tube
and sepals scarlet, large single flowers, very vigorous upright habit that
needs pinching back early, best as a
garden plant, Fairly hardy, can be
trained as a standard or pyramid or
used as summer bedding.
F. 'Caledonia', Lemoine, France 1899,
[a *F. magellanica* var. *gracilis* hybrid],
corolla crimson, tube and sepals
cerise, small single flowers, upright
dwarf habit, best grown in a small

container or, as it is Fairly hardy, in
the garden in sheltered areas where
it can be grown as a low hedge.
F. 'Casper Hauser', Springer, Holland
1983, corolla dark red with a black
edge to each petal, tube and sepals
scarlet, light green foliage with red
stalks, small double flowers, a
strongly growing variety with a well-
branched habit, free flowering.
F. 'Danny Boy', Tiret, USA 1961,
corolla dark red, tube and sepals pale
red, large dark green foliage, large
double flowers, upright bush habit,
self branching but needs staking and
pinching as it's blooms weigh it down.
F. 'Empress of Prussia' (AGM),

Hoppe, UK 1868, corolla magenta to
scarlet, tube and sepals scarlet, large
single flowers, upright bushy habit
with thick stems, self branching and
free flowering, best grown as a bush,
Fairly hardy.
F. 'Flash' (AGM), Hazard and Hazard,
USA 1930, corolla magenta ageing to
red, tube and sepals light magenta,
small light green foliage, small-to-
medium single flowers, very vigorous
upright bush, self branching, best
grown in a garden bed, Barely hardy
but still one of the most hardy reds,
begins flowering late.
F. 'Gartenmeister Bonstedt' (AGM),
Bonstedt, Germany 1905, corolla

Fuchsia 'Celia Smedley' (AGM)

ORIGIN: Roe, UK 1970, ['Joy Patmore' x ' Glitters'].
COROLLA COLOUR: Rich crimson with white at the base.
TUBE COLOUR: White with pink fluch.
SEPAL COLOUR: Pale rose-red.
FLOWER FORM: Single.
FLOWER SIZE: Medium.
HARDINESS: Tender to Barely hardy.

PLANT HABIT/GARDEN USES

The plant is very vigorous with an upright self-branching habit. It can grow into a large bush in the first year but benefits from cutting back in the spring when repotting or it will become bare at the base. The foliage is large and pale green with red veins. Best grown as a standard or pinch out to form a bush.

NOTABLE FEATURES

The unusual colour of the corolla and the way the sepals turn upwards make this a particularly attractive variety.

Fuchsia **'Celia Smedley'**

Fuchsia **'Mrs Lovell Swisher'**

brick red, tube and sepals brick red, the foliage is a dark bronze red, green on the upper surface and red-purple on the undersides, long triphylla type flowers, vigorous upright growth but not self branching, free flowering, best grown as a bush, very sensitive to cold so requires above average temperatures in the greenhouse in winter.

F. 'Mrs Lovell Swisher', Evans and Reeves, USA 1942, corolla dark pink, almost red, paler at the base of the petals, tube pink, sepals pink-white on top deeper on the undersides with green tips, small single flowers, vigorous upright habit, self branching, free

flowering but must be fed well, best grown as a bush, standard or as summer bedding,

F. 'Mrs W. Rundle', Rundle, UK 1883, corolla orange-crimson, tube pale rose, sepals pink with green tips, light green foliage, small (but long) single flowers, vigorous but straggly habit, does not branch readily so needs to be pinched and supported to produce an upright bush, makes a good standard, free-flowering and Barely hardy but the best flowers are produced in a greenhouse.

F. 'Northway', Golics 1976, ['La Campanella' x 'Howlett's Hardy'], corolla cherry red, tube and sepals pale pink,

small single flowers held sideways and upwards, small foliage, upright bush habit, self branching and free flowering, high nitrogen feed needed to ensure good foliage colour, a lax bush habit, best grown as a bush or in a hanging basket.

F. 'Sunset', Neiderholzer, Germany 1938, ['Rolla' x 'Aurora Superba'], corolla orange-cerise, tube light pink, sepals light pink on top, deeper pink on the undersides, green tips, foliage is light green with red veins, small-to-medium single flowers with an almost flat corolla, upright bushy growth of moderate vigour, self branching and free flowering, tolerant of bright sun.

Fuchsia 'Golden Marinka' (AGM)

ORIGIN: Weber, USA 1955, [a sport of 'Marinka'].
COROLLA COLOUR: Dark red.
TUBE COLOUR: Red.
SEPAL COLOUR: Red.
FLOWER FORM: Single.
FLOWER SIZE: Medium.
HARDINESS: Tender to Barely hardy.

PLANT HABIT/GARDEN USES

The plant has a trailing habit so is most suitable for hanging baskets. It is vigorous but easy to train and free flowering. The foliage is variegated green and yellow with red veins but requires full sun to develop the best colour. This variety can be prone to grey mould (*Botrytis*) although taking care not to overwater can minimise this.

NOTABLE FEATURES

This variety is grown for its foliage and if you like the combination of leaf variegation with red flowers, you will adore it. If not, it is a plant to which you won't give a moment's thought.

Fuchsia 'Lottie Hobby'

ORIGIN: Edward, UK 1939, [a *F. encliandra* hybrid].
COROLLA COLOUR: Scarlet.
TUBE COLOUR: Cherry red.
SEPAL COLOUR: Cherry red.
FLOWER FORM: Single.
FLOWER SIZE: Small.
HARDINESS: Barely hardy.

PLANT HABIT/GARDEN USES

A vigorous plant with an upright bushy habit. Foliage is typical of an Encliandra, being small and fern-like. The flowers, although small and late, are produced in profusion but it is a tricky plant to train. It is hardy enough to grow as a garden shrub or may be grown as a bush or quarter standard.

NOTABLE FEATURES

As with other Encliandra types, the foliage is the feature that first attracts attention.

ABOVE: *Fuchsia* 'Lottie Hobby'

LEFT: *Fuchsia* 'Golden Marinka'

Other recommended varieties

The following are all Tender to Barely hardy unless otherwise stated.

F. 'Gay Fandango', Nelson, USA 1951, corolla rose-claret, lighter at the base of the petals, tube and sepals dark pink, medium-to-large double flowers, large foliage, lax upright habit, very vigorous, free flowering, best grown as a bush or standard.

F. 'Leverkusen' (syn. 'Leverhulme'), Hartnauer, Germany 1928, [derived from a seedling of 'Andenken an Heinrich Henkel' found in 1923 in the nursery of the Bayer company], corolla salmon-carmine, tube and sepals salmon-carmine, single triphylla-type flower with a shorter tube, normal fuchsia foliage but new growth red, compact broad habit, best used as summer bedding or as a colourful container plant, flowers and buds have a tendency to drop when there are wide temperature fluctuations.

F. 'Marinka' (AGM), Rozain-Boucharlat, France 1902, corolla dark red, tube and sepals red, the foliage is dark green with red veins, medium single flowers, vigorous trailing habit, free flowering, ideal as a hanging basket plant or a weeping standard although the foliage is notoriously prone to mark if exposed to sudden cold. Half a century after its introduction, it sported to produce 'Golden Marinka' (opposite).

F. 'Mary' (AGM), Bonstedt 1894, [*F. triphylla* x *F. corymbiflora*], corolla brilliant scarlet, tube and sepals brilliant scarlet, large foliage dark green with red veins and purple shading on undersides, clusters of long single triphylla-type flowers, upright free-flowering habit, needs careful watering, a beautiful plant, combining the virtues of two wonderful parents, best grown as a bush in a container or in a greenhouse border in light shade.

F. 'Phyllis' (AGM), Brown, UK 1938, corolla rose-red, tube and sepals rose-red, small to medium single to semi-double flowers, very vigorous upright habit, free flowering, makes a standard in one season or can be grown as a bush, Barely hardy.

F. 'Red Spider', Reiter, USA 1946, corolla rose-madder, darker on the edges of the petals, tube and sepals crimson, medium single flowers, vigorous trailing habit, long branches need careful pinching in early stages, profuse flowers over a long period, best grown in a hanging basket or large container, thick foliage that is prone to red spider mite in hot weather.

F. 'Santa Cruz', Tiret, USA 1947, corolla very dark crimson, tube and sepals crimson, medium-to-large semi-double to double flowers, vigorous upright bush, free flowering, best grown as a bush or standard, Barely to Fairly hardy.

F. 'Satellite', Kennett, USA 1965, corolla dark red ageing to bright red with a pure white streak down each petal, tube green-white, sepals white with green tips, pale green foliage, large single flowers, upright bushy habit, free flowering, succulent stems prone to grey mould (*Botrytis*), best grown as a bush and stopped early, or try it as a half standard.

Fuchsia 'Rufus' (syn. 'Rufus the Red')

ORIGIN: Nelson, USA 1952.
COROLLA COLOUR: Bright red.
TUBE COLOUR: Bright red.
SEPAL COLOUR: Bright red.
FLOWER FORM: Single.
FLOWER SIZE: Medium.
HARDINESS: Barely hardy to Fairly hardy.

PLANT HABIT/GARDEN USES

A very vigorous grower with an upright bushy habit that benefits from regular pinching. It has light green foliage and a profusion of flowers. Easy to grow as a bush, standard or garden shrub in sheltered position.

NOTABLE FEATURES

A very popular variety and one that is often placed on lists of 'beginner's varieties' as it so easy and reliable.

Fuchsia 'Rufus'

Fuchsia 'Thalia' (AGM)

ORIGIN: Bonstedt, Germany 1905, [a *F. triphylla* hybrid].
COROLLA COLOUR: Orange-scarlet.
TUBE COLOUR: Deep flame red.
SEPAL COLOUR: Flame red.
FLOWER FORM: Triphylla.
FLOWER SIZE: Long.
HARDINESS: Tender to Barely hardy.

PLANT HABIT/GARDEN USES

This is a vigorous plant with an upright habit that benefits from pinching early to form a well-shaped bush. The foliage is gloriously velvety, dark olive green and has red veins and ribs. The flowers are borne in profusion in terminal racemes. An impressive summer bedding plant in a sunny position and also makes a superb specimen in a large container. One is a feature of my garden every year.

NOTABLE FEATURES

One of the most popular of the triphyllas and a plant that for many years, I considered my favourite fuchsia; it is still in my top five.

Fuchsia 'Major Heaphy'

ORIGIN: Raiser unknown.
COROLLA COLOUR: Deep brick red.
TUBE COLOUR: Red-orange.
SEPAL COLOUR: Red-orange with green tips
FLOWER FORM: Single.
FLOWER SIZE: Small.
HARDINESS: Tender to Barely hardy.

PLANT HABIT/GARDEN USES

An upright bushy plant that is self branching and free flowering. It is best grown as a bush or quarter standard.

NOTABLE FEATURES

This variety has the rather unusual and widely quoted reputation of being intolerant of drought although this is not a characteristic that I have observed.

Other recommended varieties
The following are all Tender to Barely hardy.

F. 'Torch', Munkner, USA 1963, corolla red-purple with outer petals with salmon-orange and pink markings, tube pink-white, sepals pink on top salmon pink undersides with green tips, foliage light green, medium double flowers with small petaloids, vigorous upright habit but needs pinching, free flowering, best grown as a bush or standard.
F. 'Trailing Queen', Kohene, Germany 1896, corolla dark red, tube and sepals red, foliage red-bronze, a long branching habit that needs pinching, free flowering, best grown in a hanging basket.
F. 'Trumpeter', Reiter, USA 1946, corolla salmon pink, tube and sepals salmon pink, long single triphylla flowers, foliage blue-green, a natural trailing habit with long branches and wiry stems, best grown in a hanging basket.

Fuchsia 'Thalia'

VARIETIES WITH MAINLY ORANGE PETALS

Although orange might not seem very far removed from red, in reality, real, clear orange has proved a difficult colour to achieve in fuchsias. It's also, in many ways, a fairly modern colour although breeders in the 19th and early 20th centuries did make some interesting progress: the British breeder James Lye (especially with 'Lye's Unique') and the German Carl Bonstedt (who specialised in breeding from Fuchsia triphylla*) were particularly successful.*

Fuchsia 'Lye's Unique'

ORIGIN: Lye, UK 1886.
COROLLA COLOUR: Salmon-orange.
TUBE COLOUR: White.
SEPAL COLOUR: White.
FLOWER FORM: Single.
FLOWER SIZE: Medium.
HARDINESS: Tender to Barely hardy.

PLANT HABIT/GARDEN USES

The plant is vigorous with an upright habit and dark green foliage. It is self branching and free flowering and is an excellent all-round choice for exhibition, bush or standard.

NOTABLE FEATURES

The waxy-textured, firm tube and sepals with a striking colour combine to make these flowers both beautiful and durable.

Fuchsia 'Orange Mirage'

ORIGIN: Tiret, USA 1970.
COROLLA COLOUR: Dull orange-red.
TUBE COLOUR: Pale salmon pink.
SEPAL COLOUR: Salmon pink with green tips.
FLOWER FORM: Single.
FLOWER SIZE: Medium to large.
HARDINESS: Tender to Barely hardy.

PLANT HABIT/GARDEN USES

A vigorous plant with a trailing habit. The foliage is a light green and the plant is free flowering. Best grown in a hanging basket.

Other recommended varieties

The following are Tender to Barely hardy.

F. 'Amy Lye', Lye, UK 1885, corolla orange to coral red, tube cream-white, sepals white with green tips and slight pink flush, the foliage is bronze-green when young ageing to dark green with red veins, vigorous upright bushy habit, needs pinching, best grown as a bush or standard.
F. 'Anita', Götz, Germany 1989, corolla bright orange, tube and sepals white, small-to-medium single flowers, strong upright habit needs pinching to form a bush, the flowers are held semi-erect and borne in profusion.

NOTABLE FEATURES

The combination of colour and flower shape is rather special.

Fuchsia 'Lyes Unique'

Fuchsia 'Orange Mirage'

Fuchsia 'Jackqueline'

ORIGIN: Oxtoby, UK 1987.
COROLLA COLOUR: Red coppery orange, darker at the edges.
TUBE COLOUR: Rich red.
SEPAL COLOUR: Rich red.
FLOWER FORM: Triphylla.
FLOWER SIZE: Medium.
HARDINESS: Tender to Barely hardy.

PLANT HABIT/GARDEN USES

This is one of the more striking triphylla varieties. Like many others of this group, it has a markedly upright habit and I use it in a large container in a narrow, sheltered and rather cool corner where it is very striking.

NOTABLE FEATURES

More richly orange than many so-called orange varieties of triphylla type so take care not to use a brick-red terracotta container.

Fuchsia 'Jackqueline'

Other recommended varieties
The following are all Tender to Barely hardy.

F. 'Applause', Stubbs, USA 1978, corolla deep orange-red, tube and sepals carmine, foliage dark green, large double flowers, very vigorous habit, upright but needs staking to support the large flowers if grown as a bush, very wide spreading corolla, for the best flower colour grow in partial shade in a container or a large hanging basket.
F. 'Bicentennial', Paskesen, USA 1976, corolla magenta, petals with orange stripes and orange petaloids, tube white or pale orange, sepals salmon-orange on top, orange beneath, medium-to-large double flowers, lax upright semi-trailing habit, can be grown as an upright shrub or used in a hanging basket if weighted or tied down, although the plant also makes a wonderful weeping standard, free flowering, the best colour in full sun. A variety named for the American bicentennial in 1976; it will be interesting to see if it manages to survive through the third century.
F. 'Chang', Hazard and Hazard, USA 1946, [a seedling of *F. cordifolia*], corolla brilliant orange, tube orange-red, sepals orange-red with green tips, foliage large and light green, small single flowers that look like small pagodas, very vigorous upright habit, needs early pinching to train it

Fuchsia 'Orange Crush'

ORIGIN: Handley, UK 1972.
COROLLA COLOUR: Bright orange, paler at the base of the petals.
TUBE COLOUR: Orange-salmon.
SEPAL COLOUR: Orange-salmon.
FLOWER FORM: Single.
FLOWER SIZE: Medium.
HARDINESS: Tender to Barely hardy.

PLANT HABIT/GARDEN USES

The plant has an upright bushy habit with short joints, and light green foliage. The flowers appear early and are borne in profusion. It is a variety tolerant of hot sun and makes a good summer bedding plant or container subject or can be grown as a standard.

NOTABLE FEATURES

Similar to 'Orange Flair', another Handley variety, but the sepals are carried horizontally.

Fuchsia 'Orange Crush'

into a recognised shape, best in the greenhouse but can be grown outside in sunny sheltered areas or grown as a standard.

F. 'Falling Stars', Reiter, USA 1941, ['Morning Mist' x 'Cascade'], corolla dark orange-red, almost brown, tube pale pink, sepals deep red-pink, foliage light green, small-to-medium single flowers, upright to lax habit, it can form a bush if pinched out early, otherwise long arching branches are produced, best grown as a bush, standard or in a container, making a feature of the unusually coloured flowers, needs a sunny position.

F. 'Fire Mountain', Stubbs, USA 1980, ['Novella' x ('Applause' x 'Bicentennial')], corolla orange-carmine, shaded orange on the outer petals, tube pink, sepals pale orange-pink, the foliage has red veins, large double flowers, semi-trailing habit can be used in a hanging baskets if weighted or tied down, on young plants the flowers may be single or semi-double, a bright sunny position is needed for the best flower colour.

F. 'Golden Dawn', Haag, USA 1951, corolla light orange, tube and sepals pale salmon pink, medium single flowers, vigorous upright bushy habit, free flowering, best grown as a bush or standard, tolerant of full sun.

F. 'Hampshire Treasure', Clark, UK 1983, corolla orange and cerise, tube and sepals pale salmon-orange, medium double flowers, upright habit, fairly vigorous, free flowering, best as a bush or quarter standard.

F. 'Stella Ann', Baker-Dunnett, UK 1974, corolla deep orange, tube scarlet, sepals coral red with green tips, the foliage is olive green with red veins and undersides, single triphylla type flower, vigorous upright bushy growth, free flowering, best grown as a bush, standard or summer bedding.

F. 'Vanessa Jackson', Handley, UK 1980, corolla salmon-orange ageing to orange-red then rich cardinal red at the edges, tube salmon-red, sepals salmon-orange, foliage tinged with bronze, large single flowers, natural trailing habit, free flowering, best grown in a hanging basket.

Fuchsia 'Tangerine'

ORIGIN: Tiret, USA 1949, [a *F. cordifolia* hybrid].
COROLLA COLOUR: Brilliant salmon-orange.
TUBE COLOUR: Deep pink.
SEPAL COLOUR: Light green with carmine flush and green tips.
FLOWER FORM: Single.
FLOWER SIZE: Medium.
HARDINESS: Tender to Barely hardy.

PLANT HABIT/GARDEN USES

A free-flowering vigorous plant with an upright habit, it needs pinching early to form a good shape. When used as summer bedding, it can attain 1-1.2m (3-4ft) in a sunny garden border but some support may be necessary as the growth tends to be soft and succulent. With its pale green foliage and paler orange colour it offers a distinctive colour combination.

NOTABLE FEATURES

Probably still the most vigorous of the orange-flowered fuchsias and also one with a particularly vivid colour.

Fuchsia 'Tangerine'

Fuchsia 'Dancing Flame'

ORIGIN: Stubbs, USA 1982, ['Novella' x 'Applause'].
COROLLA COLOUR: Orange-carmine, deeper in the centre and lighter on the undersides.
TUBE COLOUR: Pale orange to pink with darker stripes.
SEPAL COLOUR: Pale orange on top, deeper orange on the undersides.
FLOWER FORM: Double.
FLOWER SIZE: Medium.
HARDINESS: Tender to Barely hardy.

PLANT HABIT/GARDEN USES

This plant has a trailing habit so is best grown in a hanging basket although with support, it can be grown as a bush.

NOTABLE FEATURES

Like most California-bred varieties, it is a good plant for the generally increasingly warm European summers.

Fuchsia 'Dancing Flame'

Fuchsia 'Laura'

ORIGIN: Raiser unknown but probably Dutch around 1986 (although note that there are at least three other, differently coloured varieties with the same name).
COROLLA COLOUR: Dusky orange.
TUBE COLOUR: Pale orange.
SEPAL COLOUR: Pale orange.
FLOWER FORM: Single.
FLOWER SIZE: Medium.
HARDINESS: Tender to Barely hardy.

PLANT HABIT/GARDEN USES

A bushy upright, very free-flowering plant that can be grown as a bush or standard.

Other recommended varieties
The following are all Tender to Barely hardy.

F. 'Börnemanns Beste', Bonstedt, Germany 1904, orange-red, triphylla type flowers, vigorous upright growth.
F. 'Buttercup', Paskesen, USA 1976, corolla bright orange, tube and sepals soft rose pink, medium single flowers, upright bushy habit, should be grown in the shade for the best flower colour.
F. 'Claire de Lune', Rozain-Bouchar-lat, France 1880, corolla salmon-orange, tube orange-pink, sepals orange-pink with green tips, foliage large and bronze-green, large single flowers, vigorous upright bushy habit, free flowering, best grown as a bush or standard.
F. 'Coralle' (syn. 'Koralle') (AGM), Bonstedt, Germany 1905, [a F. tri-phylla hybrid], corolla salmon-orange, tube and sepals salmon-orange, foliage deep bronze-green and velvety, medium-to-long single triphylla-type flowers, upright, vigorous, free flowering over a long period, best grown as a bush.
F. 'Hinnerike', Bögemann, Germany 1984, [F. x bacillaris x F. magdalenae] corolla orange-red, tube dark red, sepals bright red, foliage glossy dark green with red veins, long, enclian-dra-type flowers, vigorous upright habit with long internodes, self

Fuchsia 'Space Shuttle'

NOTABLE FEATURES

One of the most floriferous orange fuchsias that I have grown.

Fuchsia 'Nikkis Findling'

ORIGIN: Ermel, Holland 1985.
COROLLA COLOUR: Bright orange.
TUBE COLOUR: Orange.
SEPAL COLOUR: Orange-rose pink.
FLOWER FORM: Single.
FLOWER SIZE: Medium.
HARDINESS: Tender to Barely hardy.

PLANT HABIT/GARDEN USES

This plant has an upright bushy habit with short joints. It is best grown as a bush or standard.

NOTABLE FEATURES

One of the neatest and most compact of orange varieties.

Fuchsia **'Orange Drops'**

branching but early pinching produces a better shape, free flowering, will attain 1m (3ft) in a season so best as a bush in a bed or large container.

F. 'John Maynard Scales', Goulding, UK 1985, corolla bright orange, tube and sepals orange, foliage sage green, single triphylla-type flowers, very vigorous upright habit, terminal flowers in profusion, best grown as a bush.

F. 'Lord Lonsdale', raiser and date of introduction not known, UK corolla orange-salmon, tube pale apricot pink, sepals apricot-pink with green tips, medium single flowers, foliage large and light green, when young the leaves curl and appear diseased but this is an inherent characteristic, vigorous upright habit, needs pinching

out, free flowering, succulent stalks prone to grey mould (*Botrytis*), best as a bush in a warm sunny spot.

F. 'Machu Picchu', De Graaff, Holland 1976, [a seedling from 'Speciosa'], corolla dark orange, tube and sepals salmon-orange, foliage grey-green medium single flowers, lax to upright habit with prolific flowers in clusters at the end of the shoots, best grown in a hanging basket and in warmth.

F. 'Orange Drops', Martin, USA 1963, corolla orange, tube light orange, sepals light orange with green tips, large foliage, medium single flowers in clusters, bushy upright habit but needs early and frequent pinching, free flowering, best grown as a bush, standard or in a hanging basket.

F. 'Orange Flare', Handley, UK 1972, corolla light orange at the base of the petals shading to deep orange on the outer edges, tube and sepals orange-salmon, medium single flowers, upright bushy habit, best grown as a bush, self branching and free flowering, flowers are early yet long lasting.

F. 'Space Shuttle', De Graaff, Holland 1981, ['Speciosa' x *F. splendens*], corolla light yellow with an orange base ageing to light orange, tube red, sepals red with green tips, the foliage is grey-green large and velvety, small, long-tubed single flowers, lax to upright habit that needs regular pinching and support, free flowering, vigorous so it needs a container or greenhouse.

VARIETIES WITH MAINLY BLUE PETALS

" I have included here those fuchsia varieties not covered by my descriptions under the other colours; and although most are blue, some verge on lilac or grey. Most flowers in this group, like their wonderful progenitor, 'Venus Victrix', combine blue petals with white tubes and sepals, although pink or red with blue are also fairly frequent combinations. I know of no varieties with blue petals and purple, mauve or orange tube and sepals. Like most blue flowers (and bear in mind that there is no fuchsia with a really dominant floral blue such as that found in gentians and campanulas), these flowers give a cool, restful feel to any planting. "

Fuchsia 'Blue Pearl'

ORIGIN: Martin, USA 1957.
COROLLA COLOUR: Violet-blue, pink at the base.
TUBE COLOUR: White with green flush.
SEPAL COLOUR: White with pink tinge on undersides.
FLOWER FORM: Double.
FLOWER SIZE: Large.
HARDINESS: Tender to Barely hardy.

PLANT HABIT/GARDEN USES

A vigorous variety with an upright habit although by tying or weighting, it can rather effectively be persuaded to trail. It is very easy to grow but feed well to prolong the flowering period.

NOTABLE FEATURES

The flower opens flat and each petal is finely tooth-edged, a feature that can be appreciated only if it is positioned where it can be seen at close quarters.

Fuchsia 'Blush of Dawn'

ORIGIN: Martin, USA 1962.
COROLLA COLOUR: Silver grey-lilac.
TUBE COLOUR: Green-white.
SEPAL COLOUR: White with green tips and pale pink undersides.
FLOWER FORM: Double.
FLOWER SIZE: Large.
HARDINESS: Tender to Barely hardy.

Fuchsia **'Blush of Dawn'**

PLANT HABIT/GARDEN USES

This plant is a slow grower and flowers rather late. It has a semi-trailing habit but can be grown as a bush, container plant or in a hanging basket. The flowers are very profuse and long lasting but look best in a greenhouse as they tend to be disfigured by wind and rain.

NOTABLE FEATURES

A delicately coloured variety for the greenhouse.

Fuchsia **'Blue Pearl'**

Fuchsia 'President Leo Boullemier'

ORIGIN: Burns, UK 1983, ['Joy Patmore' x 'Cloverdale Pearl'].
COROLLA COLOUR: Magenta blue ageing to blue-pink.
TUBE COLOUR: Streaked magenta.
SEPAL COLOUR: Pink-white.
FLOWER FORM: Single.
FLOWER SIZE: Medium.
HARDINESS: Barely hardy.

PLANT HABIT/GARDEN USES

The plant is very vigorous with an upright habit and free-flowering nature. The foliage is large, dark green with serrated edges. It is a variety suitable for growing as a bush or standard and is hardy enough to be a garden plant for a sheltered spot.

NOTABLE FEATURES

A vigorous and free-flowering variety; an ideal plant for the inexperienced.

Fuchsia **'President Leo Boullemier'**

Other recommended varieties
The following are Tender to Barely hardy.

F. 'Blue Veil', Pacey, UK 1980, corolla clear light blue, tube and sepals pure white, large double flowers, trailing habit, best grown in a hanging basket although I have seen one look stunning in a pot on a small stand.
F. 'Carmel Blue', Hodges, USA 1956, corolla blue ageing to purple-blue, tube white, sepals white with pink tinge, medium single flowers, a vigorous upright habit, free flowering, best grown as a bush or shrub in a cool shaded position to maintain flower colour.
F. 'Circe', Kennett, USA 1965, corolla light blue ageing to lavender, pink petaloids opening out flat, tube and sepals pale pink, large semi-double flowers, upright habit, self branching and free flowering, suitable for training in large forms such as standards.
F. 'Corsair', Kennett, USA 1965, corolla light blue ageing to light purple, white base and markings on the petals, tube green-white, sepals white with green tips, foliage dark green with red veins, double flowers, lax to upright habit, can be used as an exhibition variety if pinched early.

Fuchsia 'Cliff's Unique'

ORIGIN: Gadsby, UK 1976.
COROLLA COLOUR: Clear blue ageing to pale violet-pink.
TUBE COLOUR: Light pink.
SEPAL COLOUR: White with a pink flush and green tips.
FLOWER FORM: Double.
FLOWER SIZE: Medium.
HARDINESS: Tender to Barely hardy.

PLANT HABIT/GARDEN USES

This plant has an upright bushy habit that is self branching and free flowering. It is best grown as a bush.

NOTABLE FEATURES

The name of this variety derives not from its colour which is good although certainly not unique, but from the fact that it was the first double-flowered variety to hold its flowers partly erect.

Fuchsia 'Lena Dalton'

ORIGIN: Reimers, USA 1953.
COROLLA COLOUR: Lavender-blue ageing to pink-purple, light red veins.
TUBE COLOUR: Pale pink.
SEPAL COLOUR: Pale pink with green tips.
FLOWER FORM: Double.
FLOWER SIZE: Small to medium.
HARDINESS: Tender to Barely hardy.

PLANT HABIT/GARDEN USES

An upright bush habit that is self branching and free flowering. The foliage is small, dark green with red veins. Best as a bush or trained as a quarter standard and it also makes a good exhibition variety responding well to pinching. It is, however, prone to red spider mite attack in hot weather.

NOTABLE FEATURES

A pastel-coloured variety with very compact growth.

ABOVE: *Fuchsia* 'Lena Dalton'

LEFT: *Fuchsia* 'Cliff's Unique'

Fuchsia 'Winston Churchill' (AGM)

ORIGIN: Garson, USA 1942, from the same anglophilic American breeder who produced that other wartime classic, 'R.A.F.'
COROLLA COLOUR: Lavender-blue with pink veins and pink markings on the outer petals.
TUBE COLOUR: Pink.
SEPAL COLOUR: Pink on the top with darker undersides and green tips.
FLOWER FORM: Double.
FLOWER SIZE: Small to medium.
HARDINESS: Tender to Barely hardy.

PLANT HABIT/GARDEN USES

It has an upright bushy growth habit that is self branching and free flowering. Best grown as summer bedding, a bush or a quarter standard. It is prone to red spider mite attack in hot weather and does not overwinter easily as it requires a higher than average temperature to survive.

NOTABLE FEATURES

A compact bushy variety for a relatively cool garden; ideal for a sheltered courtyard.

Fuchsia **'Winston Churchill'**

Other recommended varieties

The following are all Tender to Barely hardy.

F. 'Dawn Star', Bellamy, UK 1985, corolla rich violet, tube pale pink-purple, sepals pale rose with green tips, large double flowers, vigorous upright habit but it trails under the weight of the flowers, free flowering, makes a good bush if pinched, or may be grown in a hanging basket or as a weeping standard.
F. 'Dulcie Elizabeth', Clyne, UK 1974, corolla lavender-blue with pink markings, tube and sepals pink-purple, medium double flowers, vigorous upright bushy habit, self branching and free flowering, flowers late, best grown as a bush or exhibition plant.
F. 'Eden Lady', Ryle, UK 1978, corolla mid-blue with rose at the base of the petals, tube pale rose, sepals pink-purple, deeper on the undersides and shading to white at the tips, medium single flowers, upright bushy habit with short joints, self branching and free flowering, a good exhibition variety, best as a bush or standard.
F. 'Fiona', Clark, UK 1958, corolla blue ageing to red-purple with white markings at the base of the petals, tube white, sepals white with green tips, medium single flowers, vigorous with long shoots so it needs plenty of space, free flowering, prone to grey mould (*Botrytis*), best as a bush or standard, grown in a greenhouse.
F. 'Hampshire Blue', Clark, UK 1983, [a sport of 'Carmel Blue'], corolla pale light blue, tube and sepals white with pink flush, medium single to semi-double flowers, vigorous upright habit, free flowering, best grown as a bush or small standard.
F. 'Moonraker', Clitheroe, UK 1979, ['Northumbrian Belle' x 'Blush of Dawn'], corolla pale blue but fades with age, pale blue petaloids, tube white, sepals white with pink flush on the top and green tips, medium double flowers, a vigorous upright habit but needs support, free flowering, needs pinching, best grown as a bush or quarter standard in light shade.
F. 'Party Frock', Walker and Jones, USA 1953, corolla pale blue with pink-purple markings and veins, tube pink-purple, pink sepals rose with green tips, foliage dark green, medium single to semi-double flowers, vigorous upright growth, free flowering, best as a bush or standard.
F. 'Quasar', Walker, USA 1974, corolla violet shading to white at the base of the petals, tube and sepals white, foliage light green, large double flowers, vigorous trailing habit, free flowering, best in a hanging basket.

Fuchsia 'Dark Eyes' (AGM)

ORIGIN: Erickson, USA 1958.
COROLLA COLOUR: Deep violet-blue with a red patch at the base of the petals.
TUBE COLOUR: Deep red.
SEPAL COLOUR: Deep red.
FLOWER FORM: Double.
FLOWER SIZE: Large.
HARDINESS: Tender to Barely hardy.

PLANT HABIT/GARDEN USES

A variety with an upright bushy habit and free-flowering nature. It needs some support due to the profusion of large flowers. The foliage is glossy with red veins.

NOTABLE FEATURES

Beautiful camellia-like flowers with curled petals; a rich and sumptuous flower form.

Fuchsia 'Dark Eyes'

Fuchsia 'Phénoménal'

ORIGIN: Lemoine, France 1869.
COROLLA COLOUR: Indigo-blue but lighter at the base, slight red veins.
TUBE COLOUR: Scarlet.
SEPAL COLOUR: Scarlet.
FLOWER FORM: Double.
FLOWER SIZE: Large.
HARDINESS: Barely hardy to Fairly hardy.

PLANT HABIT/GARDEN USES

A vigorous plant with an upright bushy habit. Some support is needed as it is free flowering and the blooms are very large. The foliage is dark green with red veins. For the best flowers, grow it in a cool shaded position. I think this is my favourite among blue-flowered fuchsias.

NOTABLE FEATURES

Large distinctive flowers.

Fuchsia 'Phénomenal'

Other recommended varieties
The following are all Tender to Barely hardy unless otherwise stated.

F. 'Stanley Cash', Pennisi, USA 1970, corolla deep rich purple-blue, tube white, sepals white with green tips, foliage dark green, large double flowers, bushy trailing habit of moderate vigour, early and free flowering but needs frequent pinching to maintain flowering, attractive round buds but the blooms tend to discolour with age, best grown as a bush with early pinching or in a hanging basket.

F. 'Sweet Leilani', Tiret, USA 1957, corolla pale lavender-blue with pink markings on the outer petals, tube pale pink, sepal pale pink with green tips, large double flowers, upright bushy habit but it needs support as the flowers are heavy, free flowering, best grown as a bush or standard.

F. 'Tom Knights', Goulding, UK 1983, corolla lavender to dull violet, tube and sepals pink, medium single flowers, very vigorous, upright habit, self branching but needs pinching, free flowering, best grown as a bush or standard.

F. 'Tristesse', Blackwell, UK 1965, [a seedling of 'Lack Lustre'], corolla pale lilac-blue, tube pale rose, sepals pale rose with green tips, medium double flowers, upright bushy habit, self branching and free flowering, easy to grow as a bush for summer bedding or in a greenhouse.

F. 'Tuonela', Blackwell, UK 1969,

corolla pale lavender-blue with red veins and red shading at the base of the petals, tube and sepals red-pink, foliage large, medium double flowers, vigorous upright bushy habit, free flowering, easy to grow as a bush.

F. 'Venus Victrix', Gulliver, UK 1840, a wonderful and historic variety, the first white-sepalled fuchsia found (or perhaps bred) by a Mr John Gulliver 'gardener to the Reverend Marriott' of Hurstmonceux in Sussex (about whom I have been unable to discover anything more), corolla violet-purple shading to white at the base of the petals, tube white, sepals white with green tips, foliage small, small single flowers, upright habit, Barely hardy to Fairly hardy but slow growing and difficult, not free flowering and used mainly as a breeding parent.

F. 'Blue Bush', Gadsby, UK 1970, corolla mid-blue ageing to deep violet with pink-purple veins, tube and sepals rose, medium single flowers, vigorous upright habit, self branching, Fairly hardy and suitable as a very striking hedging plant making 1.2m (4ft) in a year.

F. 'Blue Gown', Milne, UK date unknown, corolla blue ageing to purple with carmine and pink markings, tube and sepals scarlet, large double flowers, vigorous upright habit, needs staking due to the weight of the flowers, free flowering, best grown in a greenhouse.

F. 'Blue Pinwheel', Stubbs, USA 1970, corolla lavender blue with pink base, tube long, narrow, pale red, sepals pale red, medium single flowers, vigorous trailing habit, a striking plant with a wheel-like flower, good for hanging baskets, not easy to obtain.

F. 'Cloverdale Jewel', Gadsby, UK 1974, ['Cloverdale' x 'Lady Isobel Barnett'], corolla lavender-blue with rose veins ageing to violet-blue, tube and sepals pink-purple, foliage small, medium semi-double flowers, vigorous upright bushy habit, profuse flowers over a long period, easy to grow in a container or as summer bedding.

F. 'Enchanted', Tiret, UK 1951, corolla pale mid-blue with mid-pink overlay on the outer petals, tube and sepals rose, large double flowers, trailing habit, free flowering, an ideal hanging basket plant or can be trained into other shapes.

F. 'Queen of Derby', Gadsby, UK 1975, ['Rose Bower' x 'Magenta Flush'], corolla pale violet-blue with pink flush and markings, tube carmine-pink-purple, sepals carmine-pink-purple with green tips, foliage dark green, medium double flowers, upright bushy habit but then grows horizontally, free flowering, best grown in a container.

F. 'Ridestar', Blackwell, UK 1965, corolla deep lavender-blue with cerise veins and pink at the base of the petals, tube and sepals scarlet, foliage has red veins, medium double flowers, upright bushy habit, self branching and free flowering, easy to grow as a bush or standard.

F. 'Uncle Charley', Tiret, USA 1949, corolla lilac-lavender, tube and sepals rose, medium-to-large semi-double flowers, vigorous upright bushy habit, free flowering, best grown as a bush.

Fuchsia 'Wicked Queen'

ORIGIN: Tabraham, UK 1985.
COROLLA COLOUR: Deep blue-purple.
TUBE COLOUR: Red.
SEPAL COLOUR: Red.
FLOWER FORM: Double.
FLOWER SIZE: Large.
HARDINESS: Barely hardy.

PLANT HABIT/GARDEN USES

Best grown as a container plant in all except mild areas. It is very free flowering.

NOTABLE FEATURES

The effect of the very large flowers against the dark green foliage is one I find particularly striking.

Fuchsia 'Wicked Queen'

INDEX

PHOTOGRAPHIC ACKNOWLEDGMENTS

Front cover background,
bottom left and right: Octopus Publishing Group Ltd/Andrew Lawson
Back cover: Octopus Publishing Group Ltd/Peter Myers.

A-Z Botanical Collection 42 top, /Mike Danson 44, 81;

B & B Photographs Professor Stefan Buczacki 22;

Eric Crichton 35 centre left;

John Fielding 28;

Garden Picture Library /Chris Burrows 74 Top, 83 bottom right, /Christopher Fairweather 78, /Sunniva Harte 47 Centre, /Neil Holmes 83 bottom left;

Garden & Wildlife Matters 41 bottom;

Andrew Lawson 13, 14, 15, 17, 19, 21 bottom right;

Octopus Publishing Group Ltd. 9 top right, 18, 25, 26 bottom Left, 26 bottom right, 27, 30, 38 Top Centre, 41 Top, 46, 64, 67, 73 bottom left, 77 Top, 82, /Andrew Lawson 1, 2 insert top left, 5, top, 7, 12, 16, 20, 21 top right, 24, 29 top centre, 29 top right, 31 top, 31 bottom left, 34, 35 top right, 39, 40, 42 bottom, 45 top left, 45 bottom right, 50, 52, 56 bottom right, 59 top left, 60, 61 bottom, 66 bottom left, 70 bottom left, 71, 73 bottom right, 75, 77 bottom, 80 bottom left, 84 bottom left, 85, 86 bottom left, 90 bottom left, 91, 92 centre, /Peter Myers 1 bottom, 2-3, 8, 9 top centre, 9 bottom, 10, 11, 36, 37 top centre, 37 top right, 38 top right, 43 bottom, 48 bottom left, 49 bottom right, 51 bottom Left, 51 bottom right, 54 55 centre 56 bottom left, 57, 58, 61 top, 62 bottom left, 65, 66 bottom right, 68, 69 bottom right, 70 top right, 72, 76, 79 top centre, 86, 86 top 92 top right 93;

Oakleigh Publications Slide Library 47 bottom centre, 74 bottom, 88 centre right, 88 bottom left, 89;

Photos Horticultural 32, 33, 43 top, 53 top right, 55 bottom right, 62 bottom right, 63, 69 bottom left, 79 top right, 91 bottom right;

Harry Smith Collection 48 bottom right, 53 top left, 59 bottom left, 80 bottom right, 84 bottom left